Lou Schulist always considered himself ordinary. He had no great expectations other than to live an honest and simple life patterned after his parents'. Lou was struck by how, "things," not of his own planning, made his life anything but simple and ordinary. He liked everyone and was in turn well liked. Throughout his life, without seeking stature, he either evolved into, or was selected for, leadership roles. He valued living life and refused to waste precious time, trying to accumulate wealth beyond his simple needs. Lou had faith that his real needs would always be provided, and they always were.

Lou resides at his home in Holland, Michigan, and still enjoys traveling and fishing in his beloved Michigan.

Dedication

To my dear wife, Brigitte, and the four wonderful children she gave me.

To the men and women who served and are serving our country in the military.

To the dedicated people, who worked with me, over the years, on various teams to design, manufacture and ship great products. They were highly responsible for most of the success that I had.

To two great companies that gave a young man the opportunities for success.

I also dedicate this book to all the married couples who have been together long enough to know what the biblical statement, "Two become One," means. When you love, respect, and forgive one another, "One" happens and grows continually stronger.

Lou Schulist

MEANT FOR EACH OTHER

A COLD WAR SOLDIER'S STORY

AUSTIN MACAULEY PUBLISHERS™

LONDON • CAMBRIDGE • NEW YORK • SHARJAH

Ordering Information
Quantity sales: Special discounts are available on quantity purchases by corporations, associations, and others. For details, contact the publisher at the address below.

Publisher's Cataloging-in-Publication data
Schulist, Lou
Meant for Each Other

ISBN 9781649793157 (Paperback)
ISBN 9781649793171 (Hardback)
ISBN 9781649793188 (ePub e-book)

Library of Congress Control Number: 2021908785

www.austinmacauley.com/us

First Published (2021)
40 Wall Street, 33rd Floor, Suite 3302
New York, NY 10005
USA

mail-usa@austinmacauley.com
+1 (646) 5125767

Acknowledgments

My daughter, Dierdre, who, after "Mom" died, encouraged me to capture my memories to ease the loneliness.

My extended family, whose scores of uncles, aunts, and cousins taught me continuous lessons in the joys and complexities of life.

My friend, Reuben, a Vietnam era marine veteran who sat on a bar stool next to me at the VFW and often said to me, "You should write a book."

The GI Bill. The educational opportunities, and the early financial assistance, gave my life a robust foundation.

Preface

President Reagan, on his Cold War visit to West Berlin, received much praise and credit for his famous statement, "Mr. Gorbachev, tear down this wall."

Of less note, are the millions of veterans who made that statement possible. They confronted our adversaries, often face to face, around the world; both before and after that Berlin wall was erected by the communists. Those veterans, along with our close allies, secured the global front lines of democracy during the long and dangerous Cold War.

This story is dedicated to those men and women who served on active duty, both as draftees and volunteers, and who were deployed abroad during the long and uncertain Cold War years. For many, their lives were inconveniently and emotionally interrupted. For all, their lives, like mine, were changed.

This is the story of one, of those many, who served.

Looking back, I've come to realize how often unplanned circumstances, or, human interventions, or even world affairs shaped my life. Although at the time of occurrence they seemed to be random happenings, the resulting connectedness of them to my life journey is hard to deny. Someone obviously had a complex plan for my life and, it certainly wasn't me. I assumed life would just normally happen.

Now, after eighty-plus years, I can see very clearly how my life was apparently guided. I was like a carnival bumper car. As my life unfolded, I would be doing my "whatever" daily routine and there would be an intervention by someone or something that would bump me into another life-changing direction. None of it was due to any of my own planning.

I didn't have any great plans or aspirations.

My simple expectation was a high school education, a factory job like my dad, a wife and kids, a modest home, relatives and friends, hunting and fishing, maybe some travel, and regular small-town living.

But life didn't happen that simply or uneventfully.

This is not intended to be a religious story, but to ignore my faith would make the story incomplete.

The Story

March of 1936 a boy, I, Louis, was born to Felix and Regina in Muskegon, Michigan. I was their third child of ten.

In 1944, now eight years old, I was aware of the savagery of World War II. Each evening, at bedtime, our family knelt together on various pieces of living room furniture. We prayed for victory, and, for the safe return of uncles, cousins and neighbors engaged in combat in Europe, Africa, and the Pacific.

Because I knew the war was being fought far beyond our shores, I felt safe and secure in my daily life.

September of 1937, four thousand miles away across the Atlantic Ocean, a girl, Brigitte, was born to Otto and Elfriede in Berlin, Germany.

Brigitte was their third of five children.

In 1944, at seven years of age, Brigitte was living the war. Her father, in his late thirties, was conscripted from his job on the railroad and sent to infantry combat on the Russian front. Brigitte, her mother, sister, and brothers lived in constant fear of the around the clock American and British bombings, and the Russian shelling of Berlin.

World War II was in its critical stages in the 1940s.

The outcome would shape the future of the world.

Both Louis's and Brigitte's lives would be significantly impacted, both by that war, and, even more so, by its Cold War aftermath.

Brigitte and Louis were separated by four thousand miles of land and ocean. Their countries were at war with each other. Each was influenced and impacted by two quite different circumstances of life. Only God could know that somehow, someday, they would meet.

About Lou

Growing up in Muskegon, Michigan was typical mid-western, small factory town living. Being Catholics of Polish descent made our family stand out among the Protestant, mostly Dutch-descent, families of our East Muskegon neighborhood. Religious differences were a more sensitive issue in those days. Although some name calling, "cat-lickers" and "pot-lickers," occurred occasionally, during heated moments, the children of the neighborhood tolerated each other quite nicely. Over time, we became friends as we played in the vacant lots and the dirt roads that made up our Emerson Avenue neighborhood.

After many years of reflection, I have concluded that the differences between the ways we worship and believe, matter only to us limited and finite humans. I can picture the Almighty and loving God smiling at our squabbles as He opens his arms to embrace and welcome all of us.

The phrase, "No one comes to the Father except through me," doesn't preclude the distinct possibility that a loving and all-powerful Jesus has a plan to intervene somewhere in our journey between Earth and eternity. I believe He can still rescue those who just didn't have a clear understanding or opportunity to know Him.

I can picture Jesus intercepting a soul headed for eternity and saying, "You didn't know me or believe in me during your life on Earth. Here I am, in my glory. Now, seeing, you can believe, repent, and have eternal joy!"

I believe God loves and wants us all and isn't looking for technicalities to deny us salvation.

After school, the neighborhood kids lost little time in gathering in the dirt road in front of our homes. We had time before Dad got home from work and Mom had supper ready.

We would soon begin one of our many games which all had, although unwritten, hard and fast rules. Most games required strenuous running and either had someone being "it" or, we chose sides.

All ages able to run were included and there were no differentiations between boys and girls.

The games had names: *Pom-Pom pull away*, *Capture the flag*, *Duck on a rock*, *Inny-i-over*, *Ball tag*, *Hide and seek*. There were also *Jump Rope* and *Hop-Scotch* games, usually for girls.

To preserve our scuffed up, single pair of shoes, we went mostly bare foot during the summer. We ranged within an area of familiar fields, small, wooded areas, and alleys and back yards. We had favorite climbing trees which were loaded with our carved initials. Our biggest concerns were broken glass cuts, the ever-present sand burrs and, any strange dog running loose.

Two east-west and two north-south roads enclosed the area we considered to be our neighborhood. Beyond these boundaries I always felt strangely vulnerable and kept my eyes open for strange dogs and big kids. I was always ready to run for home. As we grew older, our range of comfort increased.

B-B guns were highly prized and any kid that had one was usually followed by an admiring and envious group as he hunted birds, mostly English Sparrows. The sparrows were plentiful then and were the target of choice. Perhaps that's why sparrows are no longer as plentiful.

Most boys had cap guns and holsters so, running through the neighborhood playing Cowboys and Indians or Cops and Robbers was also a popular pastime.

At supper time, or as the evening began to darken, you heard the calls of our mothers from their front porches and back doors. Every child recognized every mother's voice.

We'd reluctantly head home; tired, dusty and sweaty.

My hair, plastered with Brilliantine hair oil to hold my pompadour, would be loaded with sand. I would shake it out as best I could. That would have to suffice until our Saturday night baths.

Summer mornings, I liked to sit on our wooden back steps and feel the sun begin to heat the day. I'd think about all kinds of things. Sometimes, I'd wonder if somewhere in the whole world, there was a kid just like me who was wondering if somewhere there was a kid just like him. In mid-summer, I'd take a saltshaker out with me and check my dad's garden for an almost ripe tomato. I'd sit and slowly relish it.

We kids often heard grown-ups talk about folks coming from the "old country." My brother Phil, younger by a year and a half, asked me, "Lou, what is the old country?"

"Well," I said, "It's a place across the ocean where everything is worn out. The houses are old and the ground there is all used up and won't hardly grow anything anymore."

I didn't really know the answer and wondered about it myself but, you can't admit that to a younger brother who looks up to you, at least so far. It could be true, otherwise, why would so many leave for America?

There were many first-generation relatives and family acquaintances of European descent still preferring to converse in their native tongues.

Our Saturday evening baths took place in a metal laundry tub which sat on a couple of kitchen chairs. At the time we had no indoor plumbing.

The water was heated in a large teapot on the kitchen gas cook stove.

For the first four of us children, taking our turns, the bath water never got changed, just more hot water added as needed. We sat in the living room waiting to be called to the kitchen for our turn. First was Eleanore, then, Leonard, Louie, and lastly, little Phil. More sisters were still in the future.

When we were done, Dad and Mom would carry the heavy tub of water to the back door and empty it out in the yard.

Mom's flowers grew best in that soapy water area.

After baths, with fresh, clean pajamas, we sat in the living room and listened to our Ward's Airline radio.

WGN, *WBBM* and *WMAQ* out of Chicago had all the best of the weekend radio programs.

We were happy and contented sitting around the radio, sometimes in the dark, and listening to such radio favorites as *Lux Radio Theater*, *I Love a Mystery*, *The Squeaking*

Door, *The Great Gildersleeve*, *Our Miss Brooks*, *Life with Luigi*, *The Green Hornet*, *Boston Blackie*, *Bulldog Drummond*, and many others. As we listened, the scenes we had in our imaginations were as vivid as any movie scenes. The latest radio episodes were often the subjects of discussion among our friends.

Popcorn was a regular Saturday night treat. It was made in melted lard in a partially covered cooking pot over a kitchen stove gas burner. Mom would stand at the stove shaking the pot, so it wouldn't burn, until the corn was through popping.

Sometimes, in the winter, Dad would get us down some dried apple slices, which he had drying on newspapers on top of our kitchen cupboards. We didn't mind occasionally having to scrape off a little mold that was beginning to form on some slices.

Sunday morning, we all dressed for mass at St. Michael's church. I hoped we would not go to 10:00 am Mass because the homily was in Polish. Mom and Dad spoke and understood Polish, but we kids were bored by what was gibberish to our ears. I did love the rich harmony of the male choir at 10:00 am Mass even though most of the hymns were in Polish.

On the way to church in our 1933 Chevy sedan, we were sternly warned about the expected behavior.

Our Dutch neighbors were very devout compared to us. Much of their Sunday was spent at worship services and, our weekday playmates were restricted from coming outdoors to play.

This made our Sundays noticeably quiet days. Occasionally, Mom and Dad would send us to the Sunday matinee at the State Theater downtown.

For twenty-six cents each, we would have a nickel for bus fare each way and sixteen cents for our movie ticket. We would ride the bus there but temptation for movie candy or popcorn would always take the second nickel.

We would then have a long walk back home, discussing the movie from our separate viewpoints.

A memorable Sunday was the morning when, after we returned from morning church services, Dad turned on his favorite radio program. He liked WTMJ Milwaukee's *Sunday Morning Masters of Rhythm* followed by, the Harz Mountain Bird Seed Company's classical music, accompanied by canaries singing seemingly in harmony with the music.

This December Sunday, there was a program interruption for an important announcement, the attack on Pearl Harbor.

Dad came into the kitchen, looking serious, and announced, "Our country is at war."

Looking back, it amazes me how quickly we all, children and grown-ups, were committed to the all-out war effort.

Nothing like that sustained surge of patriotism and total commitment has occurred in our country since then.

Opposing the threat and evils of Nazism, Fascism, and the Axis Powers truly united us.

At that time, in our country, the concept of the "citizen soldier" was the law of the land.

That meant that all fit and eligible males were subject to be conscripted to serve their country. Everyone, rich or poor, was expected to answer their country's call, and they did, including the rich and the famous. Men of the rich, middle, and poorer classes served together. In this melting pot, they saw their differences and learned to work together for the benefit of all.

As a result, all families were concerned and stayed informed of our country's international involvements.

We all potentially had "blood in the game."

In later years, when our country ended the "citizen soldier" concept, something was lost, and patriotism has suffered. Our volunteers are to be honored but, the "heart" of our country is, sadly, no longer in the game as it was back then. In a ripple effect, many values of our democracy are eroding and succumbing to individual greed and the lusting for power and influence. "The common good" is now often ignored.

The draft was obviously ended, by the privileged who were in power, to ensure that in future conflicts the more privileged classes would be insulated from serving their country without having to manipulate deferments.

Now, the poorer classes, who benefit the least from democracy and capitalism, are mostly the ones who defend it. They often choose the military hoping it may be the doorway to a better life. Too often, it isn't, and their sacrifices go largely unnoticed and not genuinely appreciated.

I recall, during the early 1940s, hearing my parents discussing the daily newspaper headlines and the sobering accounts beneath them that told of the fierce battles raging in Europe and the Pacific. In the early days of the war, the news wasn't encouraging because our country wasn't really prepared.

I remember lying awake at night, wondering if my older cousins, one fighting in Europe and two on battleships in the Pacific, would be killed.

I was annoyed those nights at being kept awake by the continuous droning of tank engines being tested around the clock at the nearby military plant.

I tried burying my ears in my pillow to no avail.

And, sometimes, as I had lain awake listening, I would picture my dad in his drab, gray work clothes, that always smelled of machine oil, standing at a machine at that same plant.

Dad had always looked so tired during those war years which had demanded long hours of overtime from those who remained "on the home front" making the machines of war.

Our allies also desperately depended on our supplying them with munitions and equipment. Because America's manufacturing might was still firmly anchored in the USA, we quickly rose to the cause and became "the arsenal of democracy."

Dad was the youngest of twelve children and was born on a farm in Polonia, Wisconsin, near Stevens Point. His parents and two sisters were born in Poland. The ten brothers were all born in Wisconsin. Two of his older brothers were drafted and served in France during WWI.

One of them died, in the trenches, of the Spanish Flu.

Dad had only a third-grade education. As a young man, he worked for a while in nearby lumber camps. He came to Muskegon to find factory work. Co-workers taught him how to understand the gauges needed to do machining. My dad could read and speak both Polish and English.

Dad met and married my mom in Muskegon.

Mom came from a family of twelve also. She was born in Tovey, Illinois and had an eighth-grade education. Her father, a coal miner, came to Muskegon to escape the coal mines and the miner's union wars going on in Taylorville, Illinois at the time.

When the effects of the depression worsened, my mom and dad and my older brother Leonard left Muskegon and went to live with Dad's parents on their Wisconsin farm, until things got better. There, my older sister, Eleanore, was born.

President Roosevelt's Federal programs like the *Civilian Conservation Corp.* and *Works Progress Administration* apparently were notably successful because the economy slowly began to pick up. Our family returned to Muskegon where my father quickly found employment.

The factory labor union movement became strong in Muskegon. As a result, wages and job security improved to where my father made a down payment on the two-story home where I was born and raised. The home still stands and houses a family.

In all my adult working years, I was employed in the engineering and management side of business. I never belonged to a union. Sitting in on various levels of management strategy meetings, however, showed me how critical the labor unions were to labor's well-being.

Professional management, whose salaries and bonuses were based on profits, strove vigorously to minimize wages and benefits. In non-union shops, it was only the threat of the union that kept wages and benefits competitive.

As a young boy, listening to the horror stories of working life prior to the emergence of unions, I could understand the strong union loyalty in Muskegon. This generation is innocently ignorant of the exploitation of labor prior to the, sometimes bloody, struggles of the union movement.

Unions soon got a bad name when some greedy Union officials began stealing Union funds for their own enrichment. In fact, it was not unlike other "White Collar" thefts which were and still are occurring, all over America.

I think it's undeniable that the unions were the key to an emerging middle class in America. Living wages and job security were common in the Muskegon area until around the seventies when companies began to put profits ahead of their employee's welfare.

Family owned and operated companies began hiring professional management which put profits ahead of all other considerations.

Companies soon began moving operations first to poorer states then, to poorer countries, where labor was cheaper and there was less threat of unions. We began losing the manufacturing capacity that, in the forties and fifties, had made us the crucial "arsenal of democracy."

As WWII raged on, we kids started a new game. We played *Army* with sergeants, corporals, and privates. Our rank was dependent mostly on our age and size.

One Sunday morning, in church, there was a loud clunk in the pew our family occupied. My mom looked at the small Cinnamon can filled with sand which had fallen out of my little brother Phil's pocket.

"What in the world is that?" Mom whispered.

Little Phil picked it up and whispered back, "My hand grenade."

I attended Oak View public school for kindergarten and for first and second grades. In kindergarten, I had my first awakening that girls are special. As I sat on my little rug, I glanced to my side and saw a pretty, blond-haired, blue-eyed girl. She smiled at me and soon, we were holding hands.

I remember a happy feeling of contentment.
Our teacher noticed and must have thought we looked cute. She gave us each a chalk eraser, and a note, and told us to hold hands and take the erasers to the janitor for him to clean.

The janitor read the note, smiled, and wrote something back on the note. He clapped the erasers together, handed the erasers and the note back to us, and sent us back to kindergarten. Even at five years of age, I thought the episode strange. I could have cleaned the erasers myself.

Beginning with the fourth grade, my parents sent me to St. Michael's parish school, about four miles away. I walked with my older brother and sister unless the snow or rain was too intense in which case, we rode the peoples transport bus system for five cents each way.

Most of the kids at St. Mike's had started in first grade so I was the new kid and drew extra attention.

At lunch time, stocky Bobbie B. passed slowly by my desk and announced in a low, menacing voice, "You and me got a fight on our hands."

Why? I wondered.

News like that travels fast and, after school, a crowd of kids were waiting for me in an empty lot nearby.

Bobbie threw the first punch.

I lowered my head, waded in, and began punching with both hands, like my mom punched the rising dough when she made homemade bread.

I must have surprised Bobby because he quickly put up both hands and said, "OK, enough," which was fine with me. We soon became after school friends.

World War II was now being waged around the globe. We prayed for our neighbors and relatives who were in the battles, we practiced hiding under our school desks in case of air raids, and we saved everything possible for the war effort.

We had a neighborhood air raid warden who would make sure all was dark during air raid practice. A knock on the door would be followed by a terse order to correct an offending leakage of light. We followed closely, news reports of allied and enemy bombings and of our gains and losses in Europe and the Pacific.

We heard the, around the clock, steady droning of nearby factories which were building and testing tank, jeep, and aircraft engines. All our local factories were converted to wartime production. We all sensed the dedicated commitment, urgency, and the all-out effort to supply our troops and allies and win the war.

Our neighborhood families, which were all mostly poor and still suffering the effects of the Great Depression, suddenly found life improving. Our dad's paychecks, enriched with union negotiated overtime pay, began to make the rationed and scarce essentials of life at least affordable if not readily available.

Rationing, of things vital to the war effort; including such things as meat, butter, gas, and rubber was serious business. Ration cheating was punishable by ten thousand-dollar fines and ten-year prison sentences.

With improving incomes, families began filling stamp books with low cost "savings stamps" in hopes of accumulating enough to trade in for an interest bearing "War Bond."

With most of the male population away at war, there was a shortage of farm workers. A volunteer program was started.

I, with my older brother Len, and sister Eleanore, walked every weekday to the Muskegon courthouse to volunteer.

There, local truck farmers took us on the back of pickups to work on their farms. We were proudly called "Victory Farm Volunteers."

At age eight, I lied my age as ten, the minimum age they would take. Frequently, I was rejected and had to walk back home, alone, carrying my tin lunch bucket.

A typical day's pay was a treasured dime or quarter because we were primarily patriotic volunteers.

Eventually, some farm help began showing up in the form of captured German prisoners. My young, buxom,

Aunt Elsie couldn't resist making eyes and flirting with the young, handsome, and friendly German prisoners.

Elsie got a verbal tongue lashing from my grandma when my brother Leonard told Grandma that Elsie spent the day sitting in the shade and flirting with the prisoners who seemed in no hurry to escape and find their way back to battle.

It's strange to think that the Japanese American families, that were incarcerated in the detention camps around the US, were treated the same as, if not in some cases worse than, our German prisoners. This, even though almost all of them were U.S. born citizens.

My brother-in-law, Miki, recalls the trauma he suffered as a young boy. He and his family were living a happy and productive life in Santa Maria, California. They were suddenly ordered out of their home, allowed one suitcase each, and placed in what Miki describes as a concentration camp in Manzanar, California. They were in family barracks, surrounded by barbed wire and guarded by armed guards in Guard towers. Within several short weeks the family went from complete freedom to total imprisonment.

It is a dark cloud on America's history and a lesson against extreme reaction to fear.

We despised the Nazis and the Japanese. We would never have anticipated that Germany and Japan would eventually become close and important allies as new and dangerous adversaries would soon emerge on the world scene. We were more hostile to the Japanese, probably because they looked different and were such tenacious fighters. Besides, we knew many friends and neighbors of German descent.

Our efforts to destroy these former enemies would soon be re-directed to re-building their countries and helping them to become democracies and, loyal allies.

Victory in Europe and the first atom bombs dropped on Japan brought World War II to a close. We all celebrated and looked forward to a time of peace and prosperity.

It soon became apparent, however, that Russia would not honor their agreement to allow free elections in the Eastern European countries that Russia occupied.

As Winston Churchill proclaimed it, *"An Iron Curtain has fallen across Eastern Europe."*

The US and its Western allies prepared to defend their boarders with Russian-controlled Eastern Europe.

The Cold War had begun along with the nuclear arms race.

During WWII, we practiced hiding under our desks in case of a bomb attack. That seemed hopeless now with "A-bombs."

Some families and communities began to build and stock below ground shelters for Atomic Bomb survival.

The seventh and eighth grades at St. Michael school were both memorable and formative in my life. Both grades shared the same classroom. We classmates, boys and girls, bonded together, probably to help each other to survive our beloved Sister Mary Stanislaus, and, to experience together our journey into becoming adolescents.

Sister Stanislaus taught both grades and all subjects.

There was warmth with frequent stern discipline.

We were drilled relentlessly in math, English, literature, spelling, history, geography and religion.

I later coasted through high school and several years of G.I. Bill college classes, mostly on my basic seventh and eighth grade learning and discipline. I'm forever thankful for it.

Looking back, it's obvious to me that the most meaningful aspect of my education was attending a Christian school.

The intertwining of scripture and prayer in my learning firmly established a lasting connection with faith that influenced me my entire life. My established trust in God gave me a sub-conscious lifelong assurance that everything would work out okay. The habit of attending Sunday church services remained with me all my life and was as natural an activity as going to work during the weekdays.

Throughout my life, I clung to the faith that my parents instilled in me both by example and, by providing for a Christian education. For a factory worker to send eight children to a non-public school seems improbable, but this was a parish school supported primarily by the congregation's weekly donations. Having Nuns as teachers was also cost effective. It was a testimony to my parents' faith. *"Do what you believe is right and things will work out for the best."*

It was a faith that began for me early and quite simply. Near our front entrance door, a picture hung on the wall. It was in an oval frame that looked to me like polished stone. It was a picture of a man in a robe kneeling, hands folded, at a large boulder and looking upward.

I was four or five years old and was standing there looking at the picture one day when my dad happened to be nearby. I asked, "Dad, who is that man and why do we have his picture hanging there?"

My dad drew up a chair, sat down, and looked at the picture with me.

"That man is named Jesus," he said. "He is the son of God, who made the world, the stars, the heavens, and all living things. God is in a place called heaven. God sent his only son, Jesus, to save the people of the world from punishment for the bad things they do here on earth.

"Jesus knew that he would soon have to die a painful death as punishment to make up for our bad things. He is praying there that God will see Him through his suffering. He is praying so hard that he is sweating drops of blood."

Dad explained, "We have the picture to remind us that Jesus saved us through his suffering and death so that when we die, if we believe in God and His son, Jesus, we can live with Him forever in Heaven."

The, "sweating drops of blood," impressed my young mind the most and, that picture is still burned into my mind.

In 1950, after a short period of uncertain peace, the Korean Conflict began and again our American military forces were in combat. A new group of young, American "Citizen Soldiers" were called away from their civilian pursuits to go fight, suffer, and many, to die in a faraway foreign land.

This war was called a "Police Action" to contain and check the spread of Communism.

Public support for the Korean war was lukewarm compared to WWII which had ended only five years earlier.

Many Americans had difficulty in seeing Communist North Korea's invasion of our ally, South Korea, as our concern.

But we, and our close allies, were committed to stop the spread of communism so we entered the costly war.

While the war raged, I graduated the eighth grade and went on to St Mary's High School. We seamlessly switched from Sisters of Mercy teachers to Dominican Sisters.

The discipline and dedication to learning continued intact and the fires of faith were continuously stoked. As in grade school, we began each day with an early morning mass service.

I skipped school the opening day of Deer hunting season, not an acceptable excuse for absence. My disciplinary assignment was to stay after classes, one hour, for five days.

Because "An idle mind is the devil's workshop," I was assigned to clean the inside of the windows on the second floor.

The first large windowpane, weakened with age, suddenly gave way as I worked on it. My right arm came down on the broken glass and a deep gash appeared about two inches above my wrist. It began bleeding profusely.

I clutched my cut arm with my left hand and showed it to Sister Clotilda who was busy at her desk nearby.

Sister let out a little cry and ran from the room. She returned quickly with a clean cloth and told me to use it to apply pressure.

Sister again ran out and soon returned with an older student who had a car and who was "volunteered" to take me for help.

St. Mary's School was located near downtown Muskegon, so I was soon in a doctor's office in the Hackley Bank Building.

Several waiting patients gasped as they saw the blood-soaked cloth and my bloody arm as I passed by.

A cleansing of the cut and sutures applied inside and out, along with an impressive bandage, transformed me from a concerned kid to a "one day hero" to the other students the next day.

Sister Clotilda decided that I had, "suffered enough" and my after-school sentence was commuted.

My early teen years were busy with high school classmates and neighborhood friends. We spent time learning to smoke cigarettes and to drink an occasional beer or wine, which we had ingenious ways of getting. Unlike WWII, we didn't pay much attention to the Korean conflict. We believed America was invincible and would soon prevail. We were wrong. The hard fought and costly war ended in a "ceasefire" which exists to this day. We did, however, save South Korea.

As teens, we hunted ducks and small game and fished all over Muskegon Lake. We spent hours trying to keep old cars and Whizzer motor bikes going. We talked about girls but were too busy for them and a little bit afraid. That was soon to change.

When we weren't otherwise busy, we hung out in our neighborhood friend Bob's family basement.

Bob's mom had died, and he lived with his dad who was always busy tending the small grocery store he owned.

Bob's elderly grandma was our, easy to fool, chaperone.

We smoked our Pall Malls and listened to Hank Snow and Eddie Arnold records knowing Grandma was too feeble to come down the basement and check on us. She would occasionally call down the steps, "Are you boys okay?"

"Yes, Grandma," we'd assure her.

The proximity of St. Mary's high school to downtown's main drag, Western Avenue, facilitated me and a friend, Andy, to land jobs as stock boys in Barker's woman's shoe store.

We'd report right after school to work several hours until closing, then, all day on Saturdays.

Back then, almost all businesses were closed and dark on Sundays.

Andy and I were quick to learn all aspects of the woman's shoes business. We rotated stock to keep the styles and sizes easy to locate numerically. We did inventories.

We put up-side down, empty shoe boxes in the shelf voids so the store would always look well stocked. When the store was extra busy, we could wait on customers.

We learned how to "turn over" a customer we were losing to a more seasoned salesperson.

We knew how to "jimmy" a shoe by slipping a cork shim under the insole to magically "find" a smaller size. Or, to make a shoe a half size bigger by taking the shoe to the back room, inserting a screw operated stretcher, and stretching it until the threads at the seams were just short of popping loose.

Sometimes my brother Phil would wait for me until the shoe store closed. He and I would then go to the nearby Elk's bowling lanes to see if we could get work setting pins.

We had to wait until the boss would know whether the regular homeless guys, who had preference, would show up.

One lucky night we both worked, until closing, racking the pin racks up and down and returning the bowling balls on the return tracks. After each throw, we'd jump down, return the ball, gather the fallen pins and place them in the rack then pull our legs up out of the way before the next ball and flying pins would come crashing into the pit. Together we earned five coveted one-dollar bills.

With our forearms black with alley dust, we walked home. We got home near midnight. The little night light on the kitchen stove glowed softly and all were asleep. Phil and I arranged and re-arranged the five one-dollar bills under the night light trying to make them look as impressive as possible. Most of our occasional, meager earnings went to the family needs. We must have been a bit too noisy. A voice came from my parents' bedroom door, "You boys get in bed."

In 1953, a new Muskegon Catholic Central High School opened, and I was in the first ever senior class. It brought together students from three local Parish high schools.

In those days, the parishes were ethnic based. St. Michael's was Polish, St. Mary's was Irish, St. Jeans was French, St. Joseph's was German, Our Lady of Grace was Italian, and Sacred Heart was Slovak.

The various ethnic groups each had their own local "hall" were meetings, wedding receptions, and ethnic celebrations were held. We'd watch the newspaper for wedding announcements and occasionally try to crash a reception in hopes of getting served a beer by an amateur bartender.

Sitting in study hall in the new high school, I noticed two girls sharing the study table with me and a classmate.

My arm accidentally touched the arm of the girl next to me.

I felt a warm glow as I looked at her and was struck by her pretty and graceful features. She was a girl of Italian descent who had transferred in from St. Joseph's High School which was near her home. She smiled at me and I was happily captured. She later admitted to experiencing similar feelings. We dated for movies and attended all the high school social functions together. I assumed I would eventually marry her.

The innocence of courtship both in dress and behavior norms in those days amazes me when measured against today's apparently relaxed standards. The woman's modest dress of those times made the "Feminine Mystique" much more mystical and magical. It is sad what womanhood has "given up" in today's competition to expose more and more of their charms.

Modesty is still attractive, mystical, magical and appealing in those females wise enough to realize it.

In my senior high school year, a dear friend from eighth grade, Marilyn, referred me for a job at her father's Standard Service Station. He needed a replacement for an employee who had been drafted for the Korean war.

Leo, the owner, interviewed me, complemented me for what I knew, and, pointing out that there was much to be learned, he hired me. Being a "gas pump jockey" in the 1950s was one of the better jobs for a high school student.

This job paid one dollar per hour which was good pay back then. It allowed me to afford my high school girlfriend.

Most of my friends stocked shelves and carried out groceries in the supermarkets for less pay and rare tips.

Leo, the boss/owner of the Standard Service station, provided us with the Standard Oil Company official uniform.

Striped trousers and the grey shirts with the Standard Oil Logo above one shirt pocket and our name above the other.

I felt cool and thought I looked sharp in the uniform.

At that time, the world didn't have enough mirrors for a young man who just couldn't get enough of admiring himself.

The girls who stopped by for gas on the way to the nearby Lake Michigan beach at Pere Marquette Park often giggled and chatted with me as I put in a dollar's worth. That was about five gallons at that time.

Because we were near the beach, young ladies often used the station's woman's restroom to change into their beach togs. We were frequently treated to a brief view of their shapely charms as they exited in their bathing suits.

Boss Leo made sure we stayed busy, pumping gas, checking oil, doing grease jobs and oil changes, cleaning the restrooms, patching tire leaks, replacing front wheel bearings and, keeping the drive, work areas, and office as spotlessly clean as possible.

My dad knew I would need reliable transportation to hold my job. I don't know how, but he and my brother Leonard showed up at the station with a two door 1947 Pontiac coupe with a straight eight engine. Dad handed me the keys with a smile.

I'm sure Dad was so pleased to be able to manage to do that for me. That car became a part of me and, a legend to this day to my still alive friends who adventured in it with me.

I was oblivious to the fact that Dad had to also pay insurance and license fees for me. He just quietly did it. Looking back, Dad did a lot, unnoticed and unappreciated by me. Moms are even more unappreciated for all they quietly do over the years.

My parents afforded me great freedom but, with the unspoken understanding that I would never bring shame to the family. My five sisters claim the three boys had it much easier than they. Maybe my dad, looking back on his own young manhood, decided his daughters needed.
closer watching.

Working in the service station helped me to keep the car running. Leo would let us work on our jalopies after the station closed for the night. One night, I and my best friend Jack worked well into the early morning hours replacing my front wheel bearings and repairing a leaky wheel brake cylinder. Around one-thirty in the morning, we were startled when the overhead bay door was thrown open and we were confronted by two policemen with guns drawn. My Standard Oil uniform helped convince the officers we were legally there. We finished, closed and went home.

6:30 am the next morning, I woke to my mom shaking me. "Leo is on the phone," she said. "He says he needs to talk to you."

I picked up the phone and heard, "Get your Pollack butt down here to the station immediately. Clean up these tools, put them away and, clean and straighten up the hoist area."

Knowing Leo, I quickly dressed, skipped breakfast, and did as he said. I got stopped on the way and given a speeding ticket for going 42 MPH in a 35 MPH zone.

Leo had a jolly way about him that both customers and employees liked and appreciated. He was a role model on honesty and, how to effectively relate with others.

I watched and learned how his personality resulted in many loyal customers. In the days of 2000 mile oil life, our grease rack was kept busy with grease jobs and oil changes.

Leo kept a card file with service records of all his local customers.

When we had a lull in business, he'd thumb through the file, find a customer he thought was probably due for service. He'd phone them and tell them his records showed that they might be due for an oil change and grease job and, that he could get them on the rack right away with no waiting. He'd offer to pick up and deliver at no added charge. It usually worked and helped keep us busy.

Leo trusted us. We had the combination to the safe and kept bills and change on our person to complete sales at the pumps. Each weekend we paid ourselves in cash.

Back in the fifties, honesty was still an expectation and an obligation.

The good mood that Leo fostered among co-workers led to a lot of back and forth teasing and occasional practical jokes. On one occasion, on my day off, I had gone out plinking with my .22 rifle. I came upon a shallow pond and from it a flock of Canadian Geese took flight. I took aim at one never expecting to hit it. Down it came. Oh my! What now?

I picked it up and put it on the floor of the back seat of my Pontiac. It stretched almost all the way across. When I showed my dad the goose and told him the story he said, "It's not open season for geese, this goose is illegal."

They raised geese on his boyhood family farm, so he said,

"I'll skin and cut it up and Mom can cook it." I said,

"I just want to quick show it to the guys at the gas station."

He said, "O.K. but hurry, I want to get the meat into the refrigerator, so it doesn't spoil."

I pulled right up to the front door of the station and honked the horn.

Leo and my co-worker Ed came out. I proudly showed them my trophy goose. Leo just shook his head and smiled. I left the goose with my dad and hurried off to pick up a couple of friends. We had plans for a movie at the drive-in theater.

I got home late in the evening. Because my dad had to get up early for work, my parents were usually in bed when I came home from my evening activities.

This evening my mom was waiting for me with a concerned look on her face.

She said, "A man called, he said he was from the Conservation Department. He said he learned that you had illegally shot a Canada goose.

"He said you need to report to the Muskegon police department tomorrow morning at 8:00 a.m."

I didn't believe it. How could they know and why would the Conservation Department send me to the police station?

I said, "Don't worry, Mom, something doesn't sound right. I need to be at work at 8:00 a.m. and that's where I'm going."

The next morning, I arrived at the station a little before 8:00. Leo looked surprised. I said, "You guys shouldn't scare my poor mom like that, I know your tricks." Leo said, "Get back in your car, you have to go to the police station and get Ed. I told him to get there before 8:00 and stop you from going in and getting into real trouble."

I went and spotted Ed sitting in his car waiting. I parked behind some parallel parked autos so I would be out of his sight. I jumped from my car and hurried to the front of the police station. As I started up the steps to the front entrance, I heard Ed's car door fly open. He shouted my name, but I ignored him and started to pull open the station door. He screamed, "Lou, stop" and came running to me.

I played dumb, (easy for me), and I said, "Ed, what are you doing here? I've got to get inside, I'm late for an appointment." Ed said, "No, no this is a joke, Leo and I set you up. Leo had me come here to stop you from going in."

I said, "It's a good one on me, but it sure worried my mom."

"Sorry, we didn't think of that," Ed replied.

Then, "We'd better get to the station." I drove slowly so he'd get there before me. When I arrived, Ed was waiting.

He said, "You Bum, I came back here all excited and laughing and telling Leo how scared you looked and how I ran and saved your butt. Leo told me you had already been here and had it all figured out."

"That's right," I said, "Don't underestimate me just because I'm a Pollack."

We all enjoyed a good laugh and Leo said, "Lou, tell your mom we're sorry, we'll try not to do something like that again."

In 1954, I graduated high school almost to my surprise. In my senior year, I had turned my energy away from being a good student and redirected it to being a young man interested in socializing. My grades suffered but apparently not enough to "do me in."

After graduation, I worked almost full time at the station. Although I was only eighteen, I became acquainted with all the older regular customers who visited at the station. One of them was a black gentleman named Jim.

Jim worked in maintenance at the nearby paper mill. He would come in every three or four weeks to fill a five gallon can with kerosene for use in cleaning equipment at the mill.

We chatted as I helped him hand pump the can full. Once, when talking about hunting, he invited me and my friend Jack to go raccoon hunting with him. It was the Fall hunting season. We fixed a Friday evening date and Jim gave me his home address. We met at Jim's home. He invited us in to meet his wife, probably to put her mind at ease. I was impressed at how tidy and welcoming their small home was.

We learned that Jim's middle-aged wife was an aide at Hackley Hospital. She greeted us warmly and told us to be careful and stay safe.

The three of us rode in Jim's pickup truck. Jim had two trained hound dogs. The two hounds rode in the bed of the truck. Jim had warned us to wear boots because we would be hunting in low ground along a creek. As we rode along, Jim told us about his two hounds named Rock and Riley.

He said Rock was a fine dog, but Riley was better. He said, "Riley corrects the errors."

Jim also said he wanted to bring along a little "fire water" but, he said, his wife told him, "No, you don't want to mislead those two young white boys."

At the site, we got out and Jim turned the hounds loose. It had become dark and in the swamp my flashlight seemed rather inadequate. Trying to keep up I almost ran broadside into a large deer standing in the swamp. It startled me and the hair stood up on my neck. I soon lost sight of the bobbing flashlights and could only hear the baying hounds.

Running through the dark woods at night, trying to follow the hounds, was tough work, tripping on roots, and getting slapped by low branches. After a long hour or so, Jim took pity on us two rookies and called in the hounds.

Riley came to his call, but Rock was somehow lost.

After calling for a while, without response, Jim said, "We'll leave Rock, I'll come back early in the morning and I expect he'll be waiting where the truck was parked."

The next time I saw Jim, he assured me that Rock was waiting the next morning and came running out of the woods as his truck pulled up.

My work schedule changed, and I wasn't working the hours when Jim came in, but boss Leo told me Jim frequently said, "Say hello to Lou," and, that Jim would comment on how much he had enjoyed "taking the two young white boys hunting."

Several local young men hung out and often met at the station which was a common thing in those days. Sunday mornings, they would come in looking for a cold 7up and to compare notes on their prior evening's adventures.

Bob, a Korean War Marine veteran, was one of the leaders of the group that gathered. Bob was wounded by a landmine in Korea and had shrapnel scars on his legs. Boss Leo got a kick out of sneaking up behind Bob, smacking the steel grease rack with a heavy hammer, and watching Bob shriek and sprint for cover.

Most of the group worked together, in construction, as brick layers for Bob's father.

Bob's dad owned a construction company and wanted Bob to quit brick laying, go to a technical school, and learn construction estimating and contract bidding.

Bob chose Chicago Technical College located on the South side of Chicago. They had the course he wanted.

Bob invited me to go with him. He would provide our transportation and lodging expense. I was flattered that Bob had asked me. Another life changing event was unexpectedly triggered.

I checked the course catalog and signed up for an affordable course in Machine Drafting and Design. I chose the course because my older brother Len was making a decent living as a draftsman at a local steel fabricating company. I thought maybe I could eventually do the same.

We found a Chicago apartment on North Kenmore avenue and began our classes in September of 1954. We traveled daily from the North side of Chicago to the South side and back using the CTA Elevated train.

Because Bob had a fiancé, we drove home to Muskegon on weekends so, Leo continued to employ me for weekends.

We also found part time jobs at Chicago's Midway Airport loading mail and luggage into the bellies of the big TWA Super Constellation airplanes. It was a strange experience lying on my back in the belly of the huge plane. The suitcases and mail bags would come through the cargo door behind my head. I would pass them over my face and body then, push them into place against the back wall with my feet.

Sitting on benches in the team room, waiting for our next plane arrival or departure assignment, we found we were different than the local lads.

They had their Chicago way of talking and seemed to not have had much experience beyond Chicago city life.

One of them once pulled out a package of Wrigley's chewing gum. He showed it to me and asked, curiously, "Do you have this kind of gum where you come from?"

We soon lost our TWA jobs because we declined to work holidays and weekends. We left Friday afternoons for Muskegon and returned Sunday evenings. Bob had his fiancé, and I needed my weekend service station wages. TWA tolerated this for a while but drew the line when we refused to work the Christmas holidays. We were told that the more senior guys had preference. When we returned after Christmas, our severance checks were waiting for us.

Classes completed, we negotiated early termination of our Chicago apartment lease and returned to Muskegon.

Bob went back to work in his father's construction business. We seldom saw each other after that because I soon was able to quit my gas station job. In February of 1955, armed with several engineering drawings from my class assignments, I went to the employment office of

Continental Motors in Muskegon. They were the major local employer and were engaged in designing and manufacturing aircraft and vehicle engines.

I was surprised when they hired me into an entry level position as a Clerk and Tracer in the Aircraft Engineering department.

When I wasn't busy filing specification books and blueprints, I was busy running up and down the four floors to the basement blueprint room getting prints run for the designers, draftsmen and checkers.

I was often complimented for my high level of service and I was hoping that I would soon be given the opportunity to begin detailing simple part changes on the drawing board.

In September of 1955, I realized most of my friends were headed to College. Continuing higher education was a financial impossibility for my parents with a family now of eight children and, I thought, I already knew enough.

I looked around the aircraft engineering department. The men were mostly at least fifty years old or more. They all treated me well, but I missed not being with guys my own age.

Search for Adventure

My closest friend Jack was working as an apprentice butcher in a local slaughterhouse. His situation was like mine; a youngster working with oldsters.

The slaughterhouse kill floor was a violent scene. Hogs would be driven into a small enclosure almost stacked on top of each other. They would each be grabbed by one hind leg which would be shackled with a chain. The chain had a hook which would be hooked on a conveyor pulling the squealing hog up onto the upper kill floor.

There, the hog's throat would be cut and allowed to bleed out before further processing. The blood drained through a hole in the concrete floor into a barrel below.

Cattle would be led onto the lower kill floor, one at a time, by a rope around the neck or horns.

The rope was fed through a steel ring on the floor and the head of the beast was pulled down until the chin touched the floor.

The kill floor butcher then expertly delivered a blow to the forehead with heavy steel mallet shaped to collapse the skull. The animal's legs immediately buckled, and it sank to the floor.

An electric hoist was then attached to the two hind legs and quickly had the animal raised for skinning, halving, and further processing.

After work, I would often visit my friend Jack at the slaughterhouse. He also worked, after regular hours, putting up meat orders for the delivery truck the next day. We chatted while he busily completed his chores, mostly working in the cooler. The sausage maker kept a salami hanging which passing workers could cut a slice from. Jack would cut me a nice slice which always hit the spot.

Before leaving, Jack would feed damp maple saw dust to the burners glowing at the base of the smokehouses, where the beautiful hams and bacon slabs hung curing in the smoke. The meat was previously injected with a curing brine to enhance the flavor.

Sometimes we would sit quietly by the smokehouse and, using a pump air gun, we would shoot the large rats which would emerge from hiding to nibble at the stacks of cracklings remaining from the rendered lard.

This particular September evening, we didn't hang around the slaughterhouse. We went to a small local store where the owner knew and trusted us enough to sell us each a quart of Pabst Blue Ribbon beer even though we were underage.

We sat in my Pontiac in front of Jack's home, each sipping our quart. Jack had brothers and sisters. They were raised by their mother because their father had died of a sudden heart attack.

Jack told me that he was going to quit the poor-paying slaughterhouse job and join the service to hopefully learn some kind of skill. I instinctively said, "I'll join too." After much talk and sips of our beers, we agreed to meet at noon the next day at the post office and enlist together in the Marines.

Jack got out of the car, got sick by the nearby school zone sign, and went into his home. I drove carefully home.

The next day, I left work at lunch time and walked down to the Post Office. Jack was waiting and we went into the Marine recruiter. He looked admiringly at Jack's strapping physique but said, "Right now, the Fleet Marine Force is over strength and we are not looking for recruits."

But he went on to say, "The Army recruiter across the hall will set you both up so you can join under the buddy system and be together for training."

We looked at each other and shrugged, "Why not" and walked across the hall.

We were somewhat disappointed because we admired our Marine veteran friends that we knew from the gas station and, we wanted to be like them.

We told the Army recruiter, we wanted to sign up for two years on the buddy system.

"No sweat," he said, which we learned was a common Army comment at that time.

Then he asked, "Are you sure you only want to do a two-year hitch? If you take three years, you have a much better chance at getting a good duty assignment."

We looked at each other, "Why not?"

We agreed and volunteered for a three-year enlistment.

I told my supervisor and co-workers at Continental Motors that I was going into the military service in about a week. They apparently took up a quick collection because a couple of days later, they presented me with a going away present.

It was a new electric shaving razor. I took it home and that night decided to try it.

To that time, I had never shaved before. I plugged it in, turned it on and ran it up the side of my face. A stinging red welt immediately appeared on my face from my jaw to my right ear. I placed the razor back in its box and put it away in the bathroom cabinet. I haven't seen it since.

Being from a large family of eight surviving children, we were all casual to each other. We may occasionally argue or disagree, and we never hugged or said, "I love you," It was just understood that we were a family.

Without fanfare, I casually told my parents that I had joined the Army and would soon be gone. They nodded and Dad said, "Are you sure of what you're doing?"

"Yes," I answered.

I guess you don't realize what a parent's feelings might be until you become one.

As my older brother, Len, shook my hand he said, "Lou, you have to be a good soldier because you are also serving for me and Phil."

My brothers both had insulin dependent Diabetes and were ineligible for military service.

When I told my girlfriend that I had enlisted in the Army, she seemed more upset that I had joined without her approval than the fact that I had done it.

I don't think it mattered much because I was appearing less and less on her social calendar. Her one Aunt had warned her not to marry me, telling her, "Lou will always be away, spending too much time hunting and fishing."

Ft. Leonard Wood, Missouri

Jack and I had our Army physicals at the Fort Wayne Induction Center in Detroit. We passed our physicals and they put us up for the night. We slept in our clothes on bunks with bare mattresses.

The next afternoon, our group of recruits were loaded in a passenger coach on a train headed for St. Louis, Missouri.

In the evening, the train stopped for a while in a small town. I went and looked out from the train platform door. I was surprised to see we'd stopped at Taylorville, Illinois.

My aunt Helen, my uncle Doug and my four older cousins lived there. The three male cousins had survived WWII combat, two on Navy ships in the Pacific, and one in the US Army infantry in Italy. Now they were back working in the Peabody Coal Mine.

I briefly thought, *Should I jump off the train and run to them?*

Too late, I had already been sworn in to serve three years. I belonged to "Uncle Sam."

At St. Louis we were moved to a car on another train.

A smartly uniformed Army MP entered and stood at the front of the car. He glared at us and we all went silent.

He let us know, in short, clipped sentences, what dire consequences we would all suffer if there was trash or damage anywhere in the train car when we reached Ft. Leonard Wood.

We believed him; although, he then immediately left the car and we never saw him again. I was impressed by his ability to obtain, and project, immediate and complete control. I can picture him in my mind to this day.

It was about 1:00 am in the morning when we arrived and got off the train. We were herded into a large room.

The NCO, who was probably called out of a warm bed to process us, did not appear at all pleased. He glared at us from under a dangling light bulb. After a long minute of silence, he bellowed out instructions on how we would be quartered for the rest of the night. His instructions were heavily laced with profanity which we soon learned was typical of army basic training communication vocabulary.

He then said, "I'm going to pass a bag among you. If you have any things or books of an embarrassing nature with you, put them in the bag. You'll be sorry if we find them later."

I was surprised how heavy the bag was when it passed by me, but I didn't dare to look in.

Our group was marched to the supply room to draw bedding. We were then directed to proceed to a nearby wooden barracks.

The Sergeant had warned us, "Absolutely no smoking."

As we were crossing a dark field with our arms full of our bedding, Jack whispered to me, "Lou, give me your bedding and carefully light us up a cigarette to share."

I did and I held the cigarette and passed it back and forth between our lips. Suddenly, a figure came racing toward us across the dark field. It was our friendly Sergeant.

His voice bellowed out, "Who the hell is smoking." Terrified, I shoved the cigarette into Jack's mouth and grabbed my bedding. If you ever smoked, you'd know how a cigarette sometimes adheres to your lip. You don't realize it until you take it away and feel it bring a piece of lip along with it.

Jack, his arms full of bedding, tried desperately to spit the cigarette butt out. It stuck to his lip.

By then, the Sergeant was at his side and, seeing Jack's dilemma, took the cigarette from his lips and ground it out under his boot. Surprisingly, no more was said, and the NCO disappeared, probably back to his warm bed for a good laugh.

Jack looked at me and said, "Thanks buddy," then, "Who the hell does that guy think he is?" We both burst out laughing.

The following morning, several hundred recruits stood in ranks. I was in the front line. Numerous individuals were singled out and sent on various work details. We were apparently killing time for several days until the next eight-week basic infantry training cycle was to begin.

The NCO in charge was standing on a raised platform overlooking the troops. He scanned the lines of soldiers-to-be and settled his gaze on me. "You look like you might have a few brains," he said, pointing to me. "Report to Building C immediately" He pointed the direction.

I found the nearby building and entered. An NCO was seated at a desk. He looked up, and I said, "Private Schulist reporting as directed, sir."

"Don't sir me," he replied. "I work for a living."

"Yes Sergeant," I answered.

I was handed a large stack of documents.

I recognized them as the multiple choice, aptitude tests we recruits had all taken earlier.

I was given a quick lesson on how to run the tests through a scanner. The resulting test score was indicated on a dial with a pointer which rotated left to right and pointed to the numerical percentage score. I interpreted the score by the pointer position and recorded it on each test paper.

The NCO watched me for several minutes, then said, "Do them all like that and place the finished, graded tests on my desk. When you're done, report back to your company area."

I thought, *oh my, all these recruit's army careers are going to depend somewhat on how accurately I score these tests.*

I guess that's how tenuous life's breaks can be. Sort of depends on how somebody, sometimes, somewhere scores our life's tests.

My buddy Jack's physical presence resulted in him getting temporary sergeant's stripes and a squad leader title.

After my brief office assignment, I was just another recruit to be harassed and whipped into shape.

Basic infantry training was a blur of class work, physical training, spit and polish, rifle and bayonet practice, long marches with weapon and field pack, and several days of bivouac in the Missouri woods.

We were constantly tired and dozed off during lectures, only to be brought quickly awake by a sharp rap of a long wooden pointer on our plastic helmet liners.

We learned how to use a gas mask, throw a hand grenade, fire a rocket launcher, and survive the infiltration course, crawling, allegedly, under live fire. "If you don't believe it, try sticking your head up." We believed it.

Several weeks into our training cycle I was approached by a recruit who introduced himself as "Tim." He explained he was drafted just as he and his fiancé were preparing for marriage. She was Catholic and Tim was taking instructions to embrace her Catholic faith. The Army chaplain had interviewed Tim and agreed he was ready for Baptism.

Tim told me he saw me in the chapel Sundays at Catholic mass. He asked me to be his baptismal Godfather. I agreed and the baptism was performed by the chaplain. Tim said he was now ready for their marriage which would occur on his first leave after basic training was done. Tim thanked me and shook my hand. I wished him well.

I never saw Tim again after basic, but I hope that he married the woman he loved and "lived happily ever after," just like in the good storybooks.

In the field, our drinking water was available in large, cylindrical, canvas bags which were called Lister bags. They were hung in various locations in the woods.

The canvas water bags each had a separate canvas cover over them and four spigots around the bottom.

I ran out of water in my canteen and went to re-fill it at the nearest Lister bag. I held my canteen at one of the spigots but just a tiny drizzle of water came out.

I tilted the bottom of the bag trying to urge a little water to the spigot. I heard a "clunk" but still no water.

I stood on tiptoe and peered in under the canvas cover. There on the inside, at the bottom of the bag, lay a large, drowned, Fox squirrel.

I emptied my canteen immediately. I reported the offending squirrel to a nearby NCO who responded with a shrug and walked away. I shrugged too and went looking for another Lister bag.

We all looked forward to daily mail call. I hoped always for a letter from my high school sweetheart. When I did get one, I'd look immediately at the closing, hoping to see it signed with, "Love." They were for a while, but the letters soon became fewer and soon were just signed.

I received one letter from my dad. In it he said, "If you must be in the Army, it's good that you are in a great outfit, The Super Sixth Armored Division."

Dad remembered it from WWII newspaper reports. My mom had to add one of her old "Polish Mother" jokes to Dad's letter.

She wrote, *PS: I was going to put in a Twenty Dollar bill for you, but Dad had already sealed the envelope. Love, Mom.*

Our final exercise was a night assault on Mt. Baldy, a hill on the vast military base. We first had to cross the Piney river on a swaying rope bridge. As I crossed the unsteady bridge and started up the hill, I heard a loud splash come from the river behind me. An observer told me to keep moving. I still wonder what ever happened to that poor recruit.

Hopefully, he was able to wade to the riverbank. I didn't hear of any drownings which would have been "big news."

We graduated from basic training and waited to learn our next assignments. I expected advanced infantry training. I was surprised to learn I was assigned to attend "The US Army Engineer School," at Ft. Belvoir, Virginia. Jack and I shook hands goodbye. The "buddy system" no longer applied. Jack was assigned to carpenter training at a base in Virginia. He was later assigned to a base in the Arctic Circle.

Ft. Belvoir, Virginia

Ft. Belvoir was quiet and relaxed compared to Ft. Leonard Wood. The training was primarily classroom work.

I was placed in a class with approximately thirty others to learn to become an "Engineer Supply Specialist."

In our class of mostly recruits there was a Master Sergeant and a Corporal who were listed as TDY or temporary duty.

They were both career soldiers who had applied for this training. I guessed it would provide them more flexibility to apply for assignments at coveted locations.

Master Sergeant Owens was put in charge of us outside the classroom and, within our assigned barracks. He was cheerful and continuously gave us the benefit of his vast experience in the US Army.

The night before our first barracks inspection, Sergeant Owens had us all scrubbing and mopping, telling us it would pay off long term because, as he said, "There's a wise, old saying, the first impression is a lasting impression."

Our barracks glistened and we passed inspection with "no gigs." We figured our first impression reputation was established and secure.

The night before our next monthly barracks inspection, Sgt. Owens again had us vigorously scrubbing and mopping.

This time he said, "There's a wise old saying, 'A new broom always sweeps clean.' We have to prove the first time wasn't just a one timer."

Obviously the "first impression" adage no longer applied.

Evenings, after class, we generally hung out on post at a beer hall near the barracks.

We took turns buying the cheap pitchers of beer that we consumed as we told mostly true stories about ourselves, and, listened to the same favorite jukebox songs over and over.

"The Yellow Rose of Texas" was the most popular at the time. The beer hall closed at 9:00 pm so we could get enough sleep to be alert at the 6:00 am wake up call.

Corporal Aguilar marched us to and from class to keep things looking military.

Aguilar was on TDY from Fort Ord in California. Being from California impressed the rest of us because he was "cool" and had all the latest cool sayings. We went out of our way to learn his quips and we were ever alert for the opportunity to use them, hopefully as casually and easily as Aguilar did.

On occasion we prowled around Washington D.C. which was known as "dog city" to the Ft. Belvoir troops. A classmate, Ken, and I had the good fortune to meet two attractive young ladies at one of the local D.C. area tourist attractions.

Ken's good looks must have attracted them because we were invited to accompany them to the one girl's home.

They both had recently graduated from a D.C. area high school.

We drank sodas and danced to record player music in the recreation room of the home.

The one girl, Sharon, told me her father worked at the Pentagon. The evening got later and, as we prepared to leave, Sharon gave me a wallet size photo, her senior class picture.

Sharon was pleasant and very pretty but because our class was nearing completion, I sensed I would never see her again.

Besides, I was still hopeful about my high school girlfriend. Sharon must have sensed my reluctance. She didn't offer her address nor suggest that we write each other.

I kissed Sharon goodbye and put the picture in my wallet. I carried it for a while and occasionally looked at it and wondered.

The November weather in Virginia was mild compared to what I was used to in Michigan. One evening I strolled out the gate to look around the local neighborhood. I spotted a small grocery store and went toward it to buy a pack of cigarettes.

I was surprised to see a sign on the front screen door, *Whites Only*. I hadn't realized that our Constitution and Bill of Rights didn't yet apply to all Americans, everywhere in the USA. Coming from Michigan, it was my first experience with overt discrimination although I had become aware that the covert type was alive up North.

We typically had weekend passes. In my class was a soldier, Ben, from Detroit, who had his own car on post.

Each Friday, immediately after class, he drove home to Detroit to be with his girlfriend.

At the time, my younger brother Phil was attending Green's Barber College in Detroit. Phil would drive back to Muskegon Friday nights to be with his girlfriend for the weekend.

We arranged it so I and another classmate, Roy, from the Muskegon area would catch a ride with Ben to the Detroit Greyhound Terminal. There, Phil would be waiting to take us home to Muskegon with him. My hopes would be to spend time with my, maybe, girlfriend. Time home was short because we had to report for class Monday morning or be AWOL.

Because we left hurriedly after the last class, we traveled, still in our fatigue uniforms.

While we watched and waited for Phil, we had to be cautious and elude the MPs who patrolled the Greyhound terminal because fatigues were forbidden in public.

The travel arrangement worked well except for a close call we had on the Pennsylvania Turnpike. Our driver Ben dozed off and we careened off the turnpike and down into the ditch along the highway. I was dozing in the back seat and heard the "click" when we took out the first road mileage marker post. I instinctively dove for the floor and wedged myself between the front and back seat.

Fortunately, the ditch was lightly covered with snow, so we slid up and down the sides without flipping over. That was lucky because we were in a convertible and there were no seat belts. A passing Semi driver with a long rope was able to ease us safely back on to the Turnpike. Our army clothes bought us some sympathy with the motorists who stopped to help.

We were given a week off for the Christmas holiday. A classmate, Stanley, from Hawaii, mentioned he could not make it home because of the short time and the expense.

My classmate, Roy, invited Stanley to come home with him for the holidays. Soon after we were home, Roy came to my home and told me his mother was not pleased that he had brought Stanley home with him. She felt the holidays should be a private family time.

My mom overheard this and said to me, "Lou, you go with Roy and get Stanley and bring him back here. On the way, stop at the store and get a big can of pineapple juice for Stanley." Mom always found room for strays.

During the holiday, I was able to spend some time with what was becoming my less ardent girlfriend.

Stanley was a big hit with my family and friends and, I came to find out later, with my girlfriend.

On the way back to Ft. Belvoir, Stanley said to me, "Lou I liked your girlfriend. She gave me a goodbye kiss that made my head spin!"

At our first pit stop, I found a phone and called my girlfriend. "Stanley told me you gave him quite a goodbye kiss."

"Well yes, I did," she replied, "He's so cute."

Stanley must have written to his mom about his visit because she wrote my mom a nice *thank you* letter. Our moms exchanged holiday greeting cards for several years.

Our class graduated in February 1956. We were to be sent to Ft. Dix, New Jersey to get our next duty assignments.

Sergeant Owens gave us our last benefit of his U.S. Army wisdom. He said, "Boys, if you are sent to Europe on a troop ship, be sure to get the top hammock so you don't get 'vominked on' by some seasick soldier."

We said our goodbyes to friends we had made in the short time we were together. I never saw nor heard from any of them again, except one.

At Ft. Dix, I was quickly processed to be sent by troop ship to Germany. My orders stated that I would be stationed in the American sector of West Berlin. After a brief overnight stay in a transient barracks, I was bussed to the waterfront of New York City. Seen through the window of the Army bus, the streets of New York City fascinated me. The city was all I imagined and more.

At the waterfront, I was directed aboard ship and was soon waving goodbye to the beautiful and inspiring Statue of Liberty.

Atlantic Crossing

I arrived by troop ship at the Port of Bremerhaven, Germany in late February of 1956 with a prayer of thanks that I would again soon be on solid ground. The February storms on the Atlantic Ocean and North Sea had tossed the troop ship, the S.S. General Hodges, continuously.

For most of the twelve-day voyage from New York, I spent my time below deck lying in my hammock hoping that the recurring waves of seasickness would eventually stop. I had heeded M.Sgt. Owens's advice and had secured a top hammock.

The smell of food at the troop's galley nauseated me so I survived on water and a box of soda crackers some sympathetic soul bought for me at the ship's store.

Each morning, we troops were all ordered out of our hammocks and outside, on deck, for fresh air and an opportunity for moving about. I spent these deck sessions lying on a large coil of rope with, what was called, "the dry heaves."

I was always thankful to return below deck where lying in my hammock made the nausea more bearable.

As I lay there, with plenty of time to think, my mind wandered back, thinking about my still young nineteen years of life. I recalled the naivety of my earlier childhood.

I had thought it was a good world. The problems were more personal, like getting sick, being broke, having bills due, and so on. That was life.

I knew people disagreed and sometimes did bad things, but I believed, in my childish mind, that every policeman was honest and kind, every soldier was brave and true, my parents knew everything, and the president of the United States was exceeded in honesty, goodness, and nobility only by God. I guess I had thought our presidents were all honorable like Lincoln and Washington, or they wouldn't be president.

I also believed that the country I lived in, The United States, truly did have "liberty and justice for all."

I remembered how difficult and disappointing it had been to have to rethink these ideals. As I grew older, I discovered, through observation and experience, that all was not as perfect as it had seemed. Now, here I was, an American soldier being sent abroad to help promote America's way of life to the rest of the world.

I felt ready to do this because I believed, even though we weren't perfect, we were by far, the best country in the world.

The twelfth day aboard the troop ship, I was suddenly shocked alert by a loud and ominous grinding sound filling the compartment. We were in the bow of the ship, so I thought at first that we had a collision.

We were quickly assured we were "just" breaking through a fresh skim ice layer in the North Sea shipping lane which was kept open by icebreakers for the Port of Bremerhaven.

As the ship approached port, my thoughts turned from days past to wondering what lies ahead now for me.

I got my duffle bag and belongings in order so I would be ready to go ashore as quickly as possible.

I knew that would be the cure for my days of seasickness.

When I disembarked from the ship, the cool, fresh, late February air was a welcome blessing, and I sensed a feeling of physical well-being return almost immediately.

Arrival in Germany

I shouldered my duffel bag, boarded a bus with the other soldiers, and was taken to a U.S. Army replacement depot in Bremen, a city nearby.

At the replacement depot, I and the other soldiers received an orientation lecture about Germany.

We were told how we, as U.S. soldiers, were expected to conduct ourselves in order to properly represent the United States, and to gain the respect and friendship of the West Germans who were now our allies.

I learned that I was one of only several GIs assigned to Germany's capital city of Berlin.

Most soldiers were replacements for the various American army units deployed along the tense, hostile border between East and West Germany.

I thought, *here I am in the country I had learned as a child to despise*. I wondered, could I now accept as a friend and ally, the once bitter enemy who had upset the lives of my family and neighbors so dramatically, and who had killed so many Americans and our allies?

Because I was bound for Berlin, I received additional special instructions. I had heard of Berlin, but I was too uninterested in politics in my teenage years to be aware that after World War II, Berlin had acquired a special status in world politics.

In my briefing, I learned that after the allied victory, Germany was divided and put under control of the four major allies.

Russia occupied and controlled the East half of Germany. The Western allies, England, France and The United States, occupied and controlled the Western half.

The understanding was that eventually free elections would be held, and a free and democratic Germany would emerge from the ruins of war.

Our ally Russia, under Stalin, intended otherwise.

A fortified dividing line, which Britain's Winston Churchill dubbed, "the Iron Curtain," was soon established between Eastern and Western Europe and across Germany between the eastern and western zones.

Russia, the one-time ally, had now become an ideological adversary. That was the essence and beginning of what was to be termed the Cold War.

The city of Berlin, where I was assigned, was located one hundred and ten miles behind this Iron Curtain, surrounded by the Russian controlled zone of East Germany.

Because Berlin had been the capital city of Nazi Germany, it was agreed that all four allies would occupy and control this important city even though it was firmly within the Soviet east zone.

Like a microcosm of Germany, the eastern half of Berlin was controlled by Russia and the western half by the three Western allies.

The Western allies separated their portion of Berlin into three sectors. A British sector, a French sector and an American sector. I was headed for the American sector.

The Western allies had immediately established a token military capability in their respective sectors to put the Russians and East Germans on notice that the Western Allies were in Berlin to stay. President Eisenhower proclaimed, "An attack on West Berlin would be considered an attack on the United States."

Berlin was a valuable outpost for Cold War espionage for both sides. The US and our allies, as well as our adversaries, had numerous "spook" operations there.

I knew now why I was being sent to Berlin, to help maintain America's Cold War advantage.

I felt proud but also a little apprehensive because it was apparent that the Western allies were hopelessly outnumbered in Berlin and surrounded by Russian and East German forces.

Through the so called, "Four Power Agreement" with Russia, the three Western allies were granted an air corridor, a rail line, and a highway route to travel through East Germany to and from their sectors of Berlin. This access was closely monitored, and continuously threatened, by the Russians.

Train to Berlin

My orders stated that I would go to Berlin by rail. I was given travel orders, which had copies both in English and Russian. I boarded the US Military train at Bremen to begin the trip which would take me through West Germany, to the border, and then, through Russian controlled Communist East Germany.

The train passed through the picturesque and orderly West German countryside.

The early signs of Spring were beginning to show in the rural areas as we continued eastward. The train arrived, and halted, at the East German border at night fall.

At the border, the train halted for formalities with the Russian officers monitoring the rail access to Berlin.

I had been given instructions, as I boarded the train, to keep the window shade of my compartment closed when we entered East Germany. It was to avoid any incident where the Russians could accuse the allies of spying and use it as an excuse to attempt to delay the train.

I was beginning to gain first-hand experience of the mistrust and tensions created by the Cold War.

I felt a sudden self-awareness and asked myself, *"How did I get into this? What am I doing here?"*

I heard shouts outside and the train began to move and slowly gain speed. I could hear the steam engine hard at work and the screeching of the steel wheels on the tracks. Although I was beginning to develop a sense of misgiving at the adventure unfolding in my life, my fatigue overcame my concerns. Following the instructions on the wall of my compartment, I converted the seat to a surprisingly comfortable sleeping berth.

The swaying of the train and the rhythmic clicking of the wheels were like a lullaby and I soon fell asleep.

The train stopped sometime during the night at a station somewhere in East Germany. The sounds outside woke me. I lay in the dark listening, trying to discern what was happening. I heard loud voices and then the shriek of the train whistle. The train again began to move.

As we slowly left the station, I looked at the dark shade covering the window. My compartment was dark inside, and I was sure I could move the shade a little and look out without being detected.

As we left the lights of the station, I half sat up and raised the corner of the shade slightly.

The train was still moving slowly. As I peered out the small opening, I saw we were moving toward a streetlamp located where a street came to an end at the railroad tracks. A fence separated the end of the street from the railroad tracks.

The dead-end street had a large circular turn-around area which was lit by the streetlamp. As far as I could see, the area outside of the circle of light was darkness.

There, in the turn-around, I witnessed a surprising sight.

A small group of uniformed Russian soldiers were gathered under the soft, yellow glow of the streetlamp. It looked almost like the setting for a theater scene.

I could see that one of the soldiers was playing a concertina although I couldn't hear it over the train noise. Several soldiers were energetically doing a type of kick dance that I had heard of and associated with the Russian culture.

The rest of the soldiers were clapping their hands, evidently to the music of the concertina which I, unfortunately, could not hear.

As the train gained speed, the soldiers passed from view, and after peering into the darkness for several minutes, I straightened the shade and lay back down.

The scene under the streetlight stayed with me and I began to think about the Russian soldiers, the first of those that I would eventually experience.

They must have been from a nearby barracks, I reasoned, but why gather at this lonely place? Was there nothing better to do? There must be a town or village nearby with a bar, music, and good German beer.

I wondered if they were volunteer soldiers, like me, restless and seeking adventure?

The rhythm of the train and the darkness once again put me to sleep.

Someone passing through the train, knocking on compartment doors, awakened me. It was daylight.

I opened my compartment door and learned that we had reached the outskirts of Berlin and would soon be at the train station.

I readied myself and waited as the train slowed and soon came to a complete halt.

I gathered my belongings and stepped off the train.

As I walked through the station, I glanced at a calendar hanging on the wall, March 3rd, 1956. At the end of the month, I would reach my twentieth birthday.

I realized that those hours on the train marked the point in my life when I left the familiar world of family, school days, and hometown friends. I was crossing over a threshold into a new phase of life. I would be fully and independently responsible for how I dealt with it.

About Brigitte

In 1942, in Berlin, Brigitte, five years old, entered kindergarten.

The kindergarten class was immunized, fed, and taught personal cleanliness including rigorous dental hygiene. Brigitte was assertive and frequently went hungry due to her adamant refusal to eat oatmeal that had husks in it.

The Nazis, now in full control of Germany, had an agenda for females. Their role was to bear and raise strong sons to serve the Reich. After Kindergarten ended, basic studies began. Brigitte's pride in herself made her a good student in her ensuing classwork. Besides the basics of reading, writing, language, and arithmetic, there was an emphasis on home economics for young school age girls.

There was an expectation for neatness and quality of homework. Brigitte spent hours on sewing assignments making sure the stitches were all straight, uniform and accurately located and properly sized and spaced.

Brigitte's father's railroad job often resulted in his being away from home for several days. This was typically train trips to the North Sea area.

Otto's age and his occupation, critical to the war effort, spared him from military service for a while. When he was home, Otto was a stern disciplinarian who demanded obedience.

Near their home was a gardening area. Otto rented a small plot of ground there where he raised rabbits, a few chickens, and, had a small vegetable and tobacco garden. Otto's children were charged with gathering grass for the rabbits and, street manure to fertilize Otto's garden. Brigitte was always embarrassed by the gathering chore but didn't dare refuse. Her older brother, Herbert, teased her saying, "Just imagine those horse droppings are apples without stems." The children tended the little farm when Otto was away on the train.

Several family tragedies occurred in quick succession at this time. Brigitte's younger brother, Manfred, was killed by a train when he ran onto the tracks to retrieve a soccer ball.

Her older brother, Herbert, was stricken with polio and was operated on to remove an atrophied leg muscle.

In their neighborhood, there were some militant Nazis who spied on neighbors and reported any activities they thought of as disloyal or questionable.

Otto was reported for using his family's rationed food allowance even though he had additional food from his small garden farm. He was reported as being seen gathering several eggs but still taking his family's egg ration amount.

Otto was adamant and unapologetic so, as the Russian counter attacks pushed the German Army back in the East, Otto was conscripted from his railroad occupation and sent to the Eastern front as an infantry soldier.

Wounded, Otto was returned to a military hospital in Berlin. Brigitte's mother, Elfriede, visited him and tended to him daily. One morning, when she arrived, she found that most of the wounded were again returned to the front in a desperate attempt to slow the Russian advance. Otto was never seen or heard from again.

He had told his wife, Elfriede, that, if sent back to the front, he would never let the Russians take him alive.

Beginning in 1943, Brigitte's school days were interrupted by the continuous bombing of Berlin by the US and Great Britain. The Berliners were now concentrating solely on survival.

Food and fuel were becoming scarce and bartering and black-market activities were becoming the rule. The family spent much of each day and night in crowded air raid shelters listening to the explosions and waiting for all clear to sound a brief reprieve. At each "all clear" they exited to observe increasing devastation and human suffering.

When possible, they scavenged for food and for fuel for the large ceramic oven which heated their third floor flat. Potato peelings, salvaged from the trash cans of more affluent neighbors were shamelessly washed clean, boiled, seasoned, and eaten.

Brigitte and Herbert, along with other street urchins, ransacked bombed out homes and businesses looking for anything of value to eat, use, or barter. Brigitte would pull along a small wagon and guard whatever Herbert could find to put in it. She had to aggressively defend it against others looking for an easy take.

In the earlier days of the bombings, efforts were made to move children outside the city and away from the danger.

Brigitte, her sister Elli, and her brother Herbert, along with their mother, Elfriede, were sent to stay with a farm family near the town of Leipzig.

Their Berlin experience of scavenging for food got Brigitte and Herbert in trouble. They found and took freshly laid eggs from barns and hen coops of nearby farmers, who soon began to realize what was happening and complained.

They also scooped a large Carp from a pond belonging to the Burgermeister of the nearby village. They hid the large fish in the farmer's barn where they were staying and ran to tell Elfriede.

When they returned to the barn, they found the farmer's cat beginning to eat the fish. They chased the cat away. Elfriede went and complained hotly to the farmer. She was hoping he might give something in compensation. He went with them to the barn to look at the fish.

"It's a big fish," he said.

"There's still enough left for you to eat,"

Elfriede replied. "You eat it," and stormed away.

As the war continued, more of Germany was coming under attack, both through the air and by ground assaults by Russia from the East and the western Allies from the West.

Brigitte's family returned to Berlin rather than chancing being over-run in the rural area and taken by Russians.

Air raid shelters, like the subway stations and building cellars, were becoming second homes. With increasing use, the shelters were deteriorating. Lice and Rats began to make an unwelcome appearance.

Life in Berlin became more dangerous as the Russians reached the outskirts, and, encountering stiff resistance, poured merciless and intense artillery fire on the city.

At the same time, the US and British air forces continued around the clock bombing of Berlin's residential areas.

Collapsed and burning buildings and, dead and wounded humans and animals, were a frequent sight as Brigitte and her family ran to and from the shelters.

Brigitte was hindered in their trips to the shelter because she felt responsible to help Herbert as he clumsily dragged his bad leg along. She hurried him along so they would reach the subway before the doors closed.

As the bombing intensity increased, it was no longer prudent to try to run to the subway shelter four blocks away.

Elfriede herded her family into the basement of the building where they lived.

Several neighbors objected saying, "You don't belong here, you always went to the subway. Go there now."

Elfriede replied, "We are residents of this building and have a right to shelter here." Elfriede was assertive by nature and forced the issue in her favor.

It was fortunate. The Russian's advance had gained them access to the subway system. Fearing armed German troops within, they flooded the closed subway. When the subway doors were opened, dead bodies were stacked where they had tried to escape from drowning in the flooded tunnels.

The Russians soon captured and occupied Berlin. For several days, the battle-weary troops were given a free run of the city. Rape and theft were commonplace. The most vicious were the soldiers from Mongolia who were serving in the Russian army.

They were mostly uneducated and less disciplined by nature of their semi-nomadic lives.

Brigitte's family and neighbors were fortunate that a Russian officer took up residence in the first floor flat of their building which, although bullet scarred, was still intact. The officer was somewhat sympathetic to the women and children inhabitants and directed the roaming enlisted soldiers away from the building.

On one occasion, when the Russian officer was away, a soldier entered the house and began going from apartment to apartment. Brigitte, now eight years old, was tucked in bed with an elderly, widowed, neighbor woman who was afraid to be alone.

The soldier pushed the apartment door open and entered the room. He walked over to the bed and ripped back the cover. As quickly as he ripped it open, the elderly lady immediately yanked the cover back over them and glared at him. The stunned soldier stood for a moment then left.

On another occasion, a Mongolian soldier accosted a woman outside the building who was pushing a baby carriage. He pulled back the baby's coverlet and spit several times on the infant. The Russian officer witnessed the event from his window. He went out and, using his side arm, shot the Mongolian and ordered his body to be taken away.

The Russians soon restored order and discipline. They began to provide the Berliners food, mostly in the form of bread and soup. Brigitte and the other urchins learned to beg the Russians for *Kleb*, the Russian word they learned for bread.

Some Russians, knowing what real hunger is, carried crusty chunks of bread with them and ripped off pieces for the begging children.

The Berliners heard that American troops would soon be entering Berlin. They waited with anticipation hoping for improved living conditions with the arrival of the Americans who they soon nick-named the *Ami's*.

When they did march in, the allied troops were welcomed by applauding Berliners. Foreign occupation was difficult to accept, but the Western allies were much preferred over the Soviet Russians.

The Russians were now forced to cede control of the western half of Berlin to the three allies.

The Berlin borough of Neukölln, where Brigitte's family lived, was in the American sector of West Berlin.

Soon, care packages with food and basic supplies began to arrive from the USA and were greatly appreciated.

Life slowly became more routine and normal. Brigitte returned to school. After several years, Brigitte reached the point where the choice had to be made between either following a college preparation route or, a trade apprenticeship. They were a working-class family so learning a trade was in order.

Brigitte's mom learned that the local butcher had an entry level opening in his shop. She urged Brigitte to apply. Brigitte was hired and began the routine. She was supplied with two sets of work apparel consisting of two each of starched, white, linen caps and aprons. Evenings, at home, Brigitte would wash, starch and iron these items, as needed, to pass a visual inspection at the shop each morning.

Brigitte was particular about her appearance and wouldn't let Elfriede freshen her shop apparel because she didn't trust Mom's dedication to exactness.

Brigitte reported, at 7:00 am, to the butcher's living quarters at the back of the shop. Her first duty each morning was to assist the butcher's wife in her morning bath, primarily washing and drying her back.

She then entered the shop and began assisting in putting out the fresh meat, sausages and cold cuts from the cooler and into the meat cases for customer viewing and selection.

At 12:00 noon, the shop would close and reopen at 3:00. Because the meat cases were ice cooled, the meat would all be returned to the cooler during the three-hour closing.

During the closing, the small staff had lunch, then, worked on sausage and cold cut making as well as refreshing the ice and tidying the meat cases. The maple butcher block, where fresh meat was cut and trimmed, was kept scraped clean when not actually in use.

Sanitation was strictly enforced, and surprise inspections were quite common.

Each weekend, the butcher made up a package of both fresh and cured meat selections for Brigitte to take home.

This aspect of Brigitte's employment arrangement was greatly appreciated and anticipated by the family.

As the months wore on, Brigitte realized she did not want to continue in the butcher trade. It did not fit her feminine persona. She began asking around among friends and neighbors about other possibilities. Her mom was not happy about possibly losing the weekly meat package.

A young woman friend came into the shop one day with exciting news. She was a seamstress in a small shop which made designer housecoats for women. She told Brigitte that the owner was going to add another sewing machine and would need another seamstress. She had quickly recommended Brigitte as a candidate for the position. Her boss agreed to interview Brigitte.

The interview was held in the owner's living quarters which were attached to the large room where the sewing machines and pattern cutting tables were located.

The other seamstresses watched from over their machines. They couldn't hear but knew their boss and could read her face and reactions.

The owner, Frau Barkow, was gracious and friendly.

She was serious, however, about determining Brigitte's suitability for learning the skills needed and, for working harmoniously with the three other seamstresses.

She obviously noted Brigitte's fresh and crisp appearance, her nicely shaped hands with trimmed, oval shaped, nails, and her fine skin and complexion which needed little or no make-up to be attractive.

Brigitte's serious but friendly attitude was an asset. Frau Barkow asked open ended questions about Brigitte's family and home life. She was pleased with Brigitte's eye contact and directness. She concluded that Brigitte would be honest, punctual, and dependable. She could be taught to be a skilled seamstress.

After an extended conversation, in which the expectations of the job were explained, Frau Barkow made an offer to Brigitte to join her staff of seamstresses at an entry level status. Brigitte happily accepted.

A new life began. Brigitte learned how to operate, clean, maintain, and properly lubricate a heavy-duty electric sewing machine. She bonded quickly with the other women.

Brigitte also learned the use of patterns and the cutting of the shapes from the expensive fabrics.

The housecoats, mostly designed by Frau Barkow, were sold at several Berlin's woman's clothing shops, which she had acquired as customers over time.

As the rookie, Brigitte was often sent to deliver orders to these shops.

She always felt self-conscious and embarrassed as she sat on the streetcar or subway train, peering through the large bundle on her lap. She felt everyone was looking at her with amusement.

One unusual errand occurred when Frau Barkow sent Brigitte searching Berlin for a phonograph record of Bing Crosby singing his hit song, *White Christmas*.

Fortunately, Brigitte found a radio shop which had received it from the USA. The Berliners were learning to appreciate American popular and classical music by listening to RIAS, Radio in the American Sector and, AFN, Armed Forces Network.

Brigitte applied herself, learned, and became a capable seamstress. Without the after hour demands of the butcher shop job, she began to realize she had more free time.

As a young woman, she felt a desire for more social life.

She, and several of her neighborhood girlfriends, began frequently crossing the border into East Berlin.

East Germany officially claimed the East German Mark exchange rate was "one for one" with the West German Mark. It couldn't be enforced on the street. The girls found that their West German money had more favorable purchasing power in the East Zone.

Although the shops in the East had less selections, the girls still looked around for bargains.

Eventually, they discovered the hangouts where the East German young adults went for relaxation, music and dancing and, they easily mixed with them.

The West Berlin young ladies sitting at their table were dressed a little more stylish and were often invited to dance.

As time passed, in West Berlin, the US Military rule against GIs fraternizing with Germans was ended.

The Allied troops were finding their way around their West Berlin sectors. Numerous bars had begun to have live music and catered to the American soldiers who had money to spend and were anxious to spend it.

Brigitte's neighborhood girlfriend, Irma, along with several girlfriends, decided to visit one of the G.I. bars.

There, Irma met and began dating an American soldier named Carmen.

Lou in Berlin 1956

I walked out of the train station onto the cobblestone streets and looked around me. This was the city of international intrigue where, for the next two and a half years, I was to experience my new life.

A small military bus was waiting to take us new arrivals to our various destinations. The American Sector of West Berlin had some specific military locations of note.

Other than the large U.S. Military Headquarters complex on Clayallee, the most notable installation was McNair Barracks which was home to the proud and ready to fight 6th Infantry Regiment.

They were notable in their dress uniforms which had the blue, braided shoulder loop.

McNair Barracks was housed in the complex which, during the war, had been Telefunkin Electronics Manufacturing.

The company had been a major contributor to supplying the German war effort.

There was also a military hospital, a tank company and a horse platoon, each having their own separate location.

I was delivered to Andrews Barracks which was in what could be called a residential type setting. It was originally the home of the German Army Officer Academy. Later, under Hitler, it became SS Troop headquarters.

Now, a U.S. military installation, Andrews Barracks was home to the 7781st Army Unit which consisted of platoons of technical services.

These were engineers, quartermaster, signal, and ordinance, platoons within what was called Service Company, Special Troops.

There was an adjacent Headquarters Company, consisting of administrative type support, sharing the same building.

Two Military Police Companies were separately located, across the parade ground, within the same compound.

I was assigned to the Engineer Platoon, Service Company, Special Troops, 7781st A.U. (army unit).

The 7781st A.U. designation was soon dropped and changed to U.S. Army Garrison, Berlin.

I reported to the First Sergeant in the Company Orderly Room. He looked at me intently for a moment.

He was probably wondering, *"Is this one going to cause me any problems?"*

He looked over a floor plan with room assignments and assigned me to a room on the second floor.

"Take your gear to your room then, go down to the quartermaster and draw your bedding and other required equipment," he said. Then, he added, "I'll have your platoon sergeant meet with you after dinner. and give you any further instructions." As I exited the orderly room, I noticed a large, framed poster on the wall across the hallway. It read:

Soldier...

Why Are You in Berlin?

TO SHOW THE BERLINERS, YOUR ALLIES, AND THE
COMMUNISTS THE BEST SOLDIERS IN OUR ARMY
TO PROTECT U.S. LIVES AND PROPERTY
TO HELP THE WEST BERLIN POLICE KEEP LAW AND
ORDER
TO FIGHT LIKE HELL, IF NECESSARY, FOR U.S.
RIGHTS AND A FREE BERLIN

The background of the poster showed a helmeted soldier standing at "present arms." Also, in the background, was the famous Berlin Brandenburg Gate separating East from West.

One of the earlier Commanding Generals of The Berlin Command had the posters made to let the troops know the expectations.

The barracks were modern and attractive. On either side of the long hallway were individual four-man rooms, each with windows along the outside wall. In my assigned room, I saw two made up bunks and two locked wall lockers.

I apparently had two roommates that I would soon meet.

I assumed that a third bunk and wall locker in the room would be mine, so I put away my belongings, got my bedding and made up my bunk. I lied down, hoping for a quick nap.

Around 5:30 that afternoon, I noticed several army buses bringing GIs back to the barracks from their various work locations. My roommates, Carmen from Camden, NJ and Bill from Minn. quickly summed up the situation and welcomed me to West Berlin. We chatted and began to get acquainted. They both had been in Berlin for about a year. Carmen worked at the Engineering Compound as a heavy equipment mechanic. Bill worked at command headquarters in the Fire Section. They invited me to go down to the mess hall with them and join them for dinner.

After going through the chow line and sitting down with my tray, I was pleased to notice that all the kitchen help were German civilians. That meant we GIs would not have to do the tedious K.P. duty. I remembered how, on K.P. duty during basic training, my fingers on both hands had gotten large water blisters. It was from the cakes of strong Lye soap used to make the soapy water I needed to wash the stacks of metal meal trays.

After dinner, my platoon sergeant met with me and informed me that I was assigned to the Engineering Clearance Section of the Post Engineers.

I would join two others working in that capacity. Although I didn't know it at that moment, it was one of the best possible duty assignments for an enlisted person in Berlin.

The three of us in the Clearance Section had a four door, compact, Ford-Taunus sedan assigned to us daily.

We had a German driver, who was familiar with West Berlin, to deliver us to and from our work assignments.

We worked by appointment either individually, or as a team, depending on our workload. Our job was to do engineering inspections of housing provided for American officers and their families, for some career NCOs and their families, and, for single officers stationed in Berlin. We also occasionally dealt with miscellaneous civilian types working with or for the US.

We wrote maintenance work orders, as needed, for repairs to heating, plumbing, electrical, etc. We also did an inspection when occupants moved out. We would then determine whether discrepancies or damages were "fair wear and tear" or due to negligence.

When we signed our inspection reports, below our signature line was the following line: "For the Commanding General, Berlin Command."

We received our appointments each morning from, and, turned in our reports at the end of our day's work to, a staff of German office workers at the Engineering Compound. They, in turn, would schedule the appropriate maintenance work and file the reports for any future reference.

They obviously cherished their jobs and meticulously performed them. They were mostly serious but friendly.

Our German colleagues were aware that we had a generous monthly cigarette allowance at the main PX. They offered to pay double our cost per carton for all that we could spare. American cigarettes were considered "the best" and somewhat of a status symbol. There seemed to be no official objection to the practice so we would sell them our excess cigarette ration to our mutual benefits.

One of the staff we worked with was an attractive young lady named Tamara. She had fled her native Russia to escape the oppression of Communism. We tried to flirt with her but to no avail, although, she was always friendly and pleasant. Tamara told us she was what was called "a White Russian." That meant her and her family had remained loyal to the Czar and against Bolshevism.   Tamara struck me as being well educated and somewhat sophisticated so I expect she was waiting to meet someone who would better fit her expectations. Maybe she was hoping for a young American or Brit with Lieutenant's bars on his shoulders.

Frequently, we might have several hours of free time between appointments. We, and our happy and willing driver, would go to a coffee shop, either at the Army Hospital or, at Tempelhof Air Base.

There, we would enjoy coffee, rolls and, whatever was being played on the jukebox. A new singing star named "Elvis" was emerging.

On one occasion, when I was working alone, the German driver invited me to join him for lunch at the Engineering Compound's German cantina.

He ordered us each a beer and a hard roll with ground raw meat on it. It was my first experience with steak tartare, and I approached it reluctantly. It was so delicious, however, that I ate it all. Later, in the car, I learned it was made of *Pferd Fleish*, which is German for horse meat. In Berlin, there were meat markets licensed to sell horse meat exclusively for human consumption.

Had I known ahead, I'm sure I would have refused. I remember my dad telling of a time on the family farm, when he and his brother were rubbing down their plow horses after a long day's work. His brother stopped, looked at my dad and commented, "How could a human being ever eat such a noble beast."

After that first experience, I was no longer reluctant, although I don't think I ever told my dad.

Sometimes, schedules permitting, we would take a ride to Wannsee, a lake which was West Berlin's bathing beach.

On warm days, we would drive slowly and admire the *Fräuleins* in their European bikinis.

On one occasion, we visited Spandau Prison, in the British sector, where five Nazi war criminals were being held.

The four occupying powers took turns, on a monthly basis, to guard the prison. We luckily witnessed the changing of the guard squads from American to Russian while we were there. It was done with military sharpness and precision.

The war criminals had served various sentences. Some served their terms and were released. Rudolf Hess had a life sentence and eventually died in Spandau. He was the last of the WWII prisoners in Spandau.

My first summer in Berlin was spent using my free time to explore the American sector. Most, Andrews Barracks GI's, began each evening outside the front gate and across the street at the *Den Goldenen Sonne*. It was a small bar with tables where the GIs would gather to start off their individual plans for the evening. A bottle of good *Berliner Kindl* beer cost 50 pfennigs, which in 1956, was 12 and 1/2 cents American. The owner, Anton, would accept our military script in payment. American "greenbacks" were not yet allowed in Berlin. Anton had a "connection" who would redeem the military script for German marks, probably for a slight fee, at the US headquarters bank.

This financial accommodation was apparently allowed, probably because it helped keep the West Berlin economy thriving.

Later, we were suddenly told that we had a short window of time to turn in our military script in exchange for "Greenbacks," real U.S. dollars. Some German proprietors were unable to unload their G.I. script fast enough and were stuck with the worthless paper.

Often, GIs would be waiting at the *Sonne* to meet their German girlfriends and to take them on post for a movie date.

After duty hours, we were typically free to be off post until midnight.

We would often hop on the streetcar which stopped just outside the gate. Usually, there were two or three of us together and we would get off the streetcar at the various places that the GIs favored.

Because Berlin had many pleasant parks and tree-lined sidewalks, we occasionally strolled. In 1956, there were still some remnants of bombed out buildings and homes.

These were typically only the foundations, still standing and neatly cleared of any debris.

In late Summer, my roommate, Bill, talked me into a plan he had to cross a bridge to the East Berlin side of Wannsee lake and to spend Saturday night at the rustic campground there.

In 1956, there was, as yet, no Berlin Wall and the Berliners could still travel freely between sectors. We requested and both got overnight passes.

Saturday, after morning roll call, we each rented a bicycle, and, equipped with our army shelter halves and sleeping bags, we headed for Wannsee.

The East Berlin side did not have the developed sandy beach that was on the West side. It was more wooded and natural and well suited for rustic camping. There we found an open campsite and joined our shelter halves together to make a two-man tent.

Tired from the long bike ride, I stretched out for a nap while Bill went for a walk along the shoreline.

Bill returned to our campsite with two smiling, young ladies. We chatted in German and English for a while.

They saw we had no food and invited us to their camp for a small picnic lunch. Along the way, we had bought some beers which we shared with the girls while we ate their hard roll and cheese sandwiches.

Bill liked the one girl and obtained her name and Berlin address. The other girl, I learned, was now a Canadian. She was born in Berlin and was back visiting her mother. The two girls were neighbors and friends from childhood.

The Canadian girl told me she got married in Canada and had become a Canadian citizen. She and her Canadian husband both worked on various merchant ships sailing throughout the Great Lakes. She was familiar with my hometown "Port of Muskegon" on Lake Michigan.

As evening approached, Bill and I came to the realization that the comforts and conveniences of barracks life were sadly missing in the East Berlin rustic campground.

We changed our minds, broke camp, said our goodbyes, and bicycled back to Andrew Barracks.

I never heard from the Canadian girl again and I assumed she soon returned to Canada and life with her husband.

Bill, however, looked up his new friend's address. Bill had only four or five months left in his enlistment, so they dated frequently until Bill returned to the USA.

My roommate Bill's duty assignment was with the Fire Department. He was part of a crew that provided around the clock fire and emergency response. Their operation was in a wing of Central Headquarters.

There was a switchboard there manned by Germans who spoke English fluently. There was a small bedroom for the American on overnight duty. And there was a fire engine red, Ford Taunus Pickup truck. It was equipped with siren, flashers and a two-way radio monitored by the Military Police and the switchboard operators.

Emergency calls would come into the switchboard operator who would notify the G.I. on duty, directly if he were present, or by radio if he were away.

The on-duty G.I. would proceed under emergency mode, if indicated by the nature of the incident, with klaxon horn and flashing emergency light, to the location and quickly evaluate the situation. Time was of the essence.

If needed, he would radio the switchboard to dispatch the German Fire Department. Calling out the Fire Department without good cause was frowned upon.

Most calls were for plumbing or electrical emergencies. The on-duty G.I. would transport the appropriate skilled maintenance help to the scene and oversee their work.

When an opening came for a replacement in the Fire Department, Bill coaxed me into bidding for it.

He talked about how great it was to have a 48-hours-on, and 48-hours-off duty cycle. I bit, applied, and was accepted.

I regretted it almost immediately. The 48 hours off was boring with everyone else away at work.

Staying in the company area left me open to harassment by NCOs, who would find odd jobs around the company area.

Overnight duty at headquarters in the small, windowless room felt like being in solitary confinement.

The only way to pass the time was reading, listening to the Armed Forces Radio Network or listening on a short-wave radio to Radio Moscow broadcasting propaganda in English. Other than the frequent routine maintenance emergencies, I had only two incidences of note.

One was a frantic call from a young wife in the NCO family housing complex. She had stepped into the hall for a moment and a breeze blew her entrance door shut.

She was locked out.

When I arrived, the woman and several neighbors were frantically standing in the hallway by the door.

They quickly explained that there was an infant baby inside and that the wife had a pot cooking on the stove.

I was familiar with the apartments from my previous job.

I was also familiar with the door locks which, when locked inside, could be opened by the inside doorknob but not by the outside knob without a key. I knew the dead bolt lock could only be locked from the inside or from outside only with a key. So, I knew that only the spring-loaded bolt was locking the door.

I got a thin screwdriver from the pick-up truck.

I lined the screwdriver point up to the left of the doorknob and gave the end of the handle a hard blow with the palm of my free hand. I applied pressure and pivoted the screwdriver handle forward in the punctured hole in the door panel. The spring bolt slid back, and the door opened. All was well inside.

The spectators in the hall looked at me with awe.

I had made it look so professional and easy. They didn't realize it was just a lucky guess and I probably couldn't make it work so easily again.

The other occasion was a call from the 6th Infantry Regiment's McNair Barracks early one evening.

The call stated two soldiers were trapped in an elevator that malfunctioned and stopped short of the floor level.

When I arrived, I quickly learned that the overhead motor had overheated and was sending acrid smoke into the shaft.

Two soldiers on a work detail had heard the trapped men banging on the elevator door and calling for help. They were standing at the elevator and had already removed the small window from the elevator door. They had reversed the hose on a large canister vacuum and were using it to force air into the car, through the opening.

I did not have the knowledge or resources to deal with the situation and I felt lives were possibly at stake.

I radioed the headquarters switchboard and said, "We have a major situation here so dispatch the German Fire Department."

All ended well. The German fire department knew what to do. They cut off power to the motor and quickly freed the two trapped soldiers.

I looked outside. Oh my gosh! Someone had pulled the fire alarm and platoons of infantry troops were standing idly outside waiting for the all- clear signal. It made the situation look worse than it was. There was soon "hell to pay."

Because I had used the words "major situation," the dispatcher notified the army Major in charge of the fire operation. The Major was called away from an Officer's social gathering and was irritated.

By the time he arrived on the scene, all was resolved, and it looked to him like over-reaction. The Major read out the German dispatcher for bothering him "unnecessarily."

I felt bad for the dispatcher because it had been my use of the word "major" that had triggered his alerting the officer. When I talked to the dispatcher about it later, he patted me on the shoulder and said, "Don't worry about it, we didn't want anyone to get hurt and so we did what we thought was right."

"By now," he said. "The Major has already forgotten about it."

We had one fatal incident during my short stay on the emergency response staff. Happily, I was off duty.

The involved G.I. a Sergeant, related the occurrence to me.

A call came in late in the evening that someone smelled smoke in the hallway of one of the apartment buildings for married NCO's. The G.I. on duty went to the location.

Entering the building, he immediately smelled the smoke. He went to the first apartment and placed his hand on the door. It was extremely hot. He immediately pulled the nearest fire alarm and radioed for the German fire Department. They were there in minutes and began spraying water on the door as they forced it opened and entered. The inside was filled with smoke and heat, but the fire was still confined to a corner of the bedroom. They quickly extinguished it but too late to save the married couple. They were lying side by side in the bed and were fatally overcome by the smoke and heat.

The sergeant said the exposed upper half of their bodies were scorched even though the blankets covering their lower halves showed no effect of the intense heat.

Acquaintances in the building said the pair were out late at an NCO dance party.

The German fire inspector said that the indications were that one of them placed a lit cigarette on the edge of the top of the dresser in the room. The cigarette, apparently forgotten, fell into a drawer of lingerie and caught fire as the couple fell quickly asleep. Actual property damage was limited to the dresser. Cigarette smoking is dangerous in many ways.

On one of my "off" days, the First Sergeant caught me at lunch in the mess hall. "When you finish lunch, come to the orderly room and see me," he said. *Caught again on my day off*, I thought, *another work detail.*

When I reported to him, he said, "Go down to the armory clerk and draw a .45 pistol and a clip of ammo. You need to go to McNair Barracks and get a man from our company who is jailed there. You will guard him and escort him to the hospital for some medical tests."

"I'm not qualified on a .45," I told him.

"What's your weapon?" he asked.

"A carbine," I replied.

"Go draw out your carbine with a clip of ammo," he told me. The Sergeant phoned down to the armory and instructed them accordingly. Military weapons and ammo were strictly controlled, unlike civilian life.

He then ordered a sedan and driver for me.

"I'll let the stockade know you're on your way," he said, "They'll instruct you further when you get there."

At the stockade they were ready for me. Being from the same company, the prisoner and I recognized each other.

The attending jailor loudly instructed me, "Put him in the front seat. You sit directly behind him in the back seat. If he tries to escape, shoot him."

Along the way to the Army hospital, the driver had to make numerous stops for cross traffic intersections.

The prisoner turned his head and said to me, "Schulist, if I opened this door and made a run for it, could you really shoot me?"

"I don't know," I replied, "Why don't you try it and we'll both find out?" Happily, he didn't try.

I was relieved to turn him over to the hospital.

I didn't understand why the MPs weren't contacted to transport him. I guessed his jail time was being kept off the record, maybe for his benefit. The Army can sometimes move in mysterious ways, I think.

Not long after, I went to the Captain in charge of my old job, the Engineering Clearance Section. I asked if I could please transfer back into my old position.

He smiled and said, "I was surprised that you transferred out of what is probably one of the best assignments for a soldier in Berlin," he went on. "The German office staff manager told me they were disappointed when you left, they enjoyed working with you."

He told me he hadn't put in a requisition for my replacement yet so he would see what he could do.

Happily, the captain got me back into my old job.

Occasionally, we were taken off our regular jobs for special projects or "hands on" engineering training.

Some of us "office types" were temporarily assigned on special projects to work along with the engineering equipment mechanics and operators who were the "real" hands on guys. We knew each other well because we shared the same barracks and were all in the Engineer Platoon.

We also hung out together outside the gate and had an unspoken understanding to take care of each other if needed. Taking care usually meant getting a comrade with too much to drink safely back to the barracks.

One such special project was to replace a stretch of barbed wire fencing in an unpopulated, remote area along the American Sector and East German border. The fence was built to prevent displaced persons and those fleeing the East from entering West Berlin without proper processing. The fence was also intended to discourage smuggling in the remote area.

The Russians monitored the area and reported that, over time, the wire fencing had deteriorated and was severely damaged. They said it needed to be replaced. They claimed it was on the US side thus, our responsibility.

At a Saturday morning platoon meeting, we were told of the unusual nature of the border project. Several seasoned career NCOs were assigned to plan the work, requisition the material and tools, and supervise the job. A mixed team of engineer GIs was chosen, and I was one of them.

We were told the Russians would be notified of our plans and that they had stated they would have guards present.

Monday morning, we loaded spools of double strand galvanized barbed wire, crowbars, post hole diggers, hammers and staples, and set out, on a bus, for the location.

Because we would be in direct presence of Russian troops, several officers accompanied us to the job site in an Army sedan.

The Soviets were previously informed that we would have a work crew at that zone border location that day.

When we got off the bus, a small number of Russian guards were spaced along their side. They were armed with automatic weapons and had several police dogs on leashes.

I laughed to myself, we were armed with crow bars and post hole diggers.

I went back to the bus and got my brand-new Retina IIIC camera. As I was headed back toward the fence area, a Major stopped me. "Soldier, what do you think you're doing?" he asked angrily.

I answered, "Sir, I want to get a couple close up pictures of the Russians."

He came up close to my face, "Do you want to start something and see us all get cut down by those Burp guns?" he asked.

I answered, "Sir, we're in our American Sector, I thought we should be able to do what we please."

The major snapped back, "Soldier, I'm ordering you to put that damn camera back on the bus immediately or I'll have you court-martialed for disobeying a direct order."

"Yes sir," I answered. I saluted, and he watched as I put the camera back on the bus. With the unpredictability of the Russians, he was probably right in his caution.

The fence was hard work, but it was satisfying to see the results as we strung the new wire. We removed the remnants of the old wire and replaced any of the ten-foot-long 4x4 fence posts that weren't still solid. Two GIs would put a crowbar through a round coil of barbed wire and walk along feeding it out along the fence line.

With our heavy leather gloves, we would pull the wire to a fence post. One man would hook a large crowbar to a barb and use it as a lever to tension the wire. Another man would drive a staple on both sides of a barb to anchor the tensioned wire to the post.

There was approximately seven feet of post above the ground and we were told to space the runs of wire approximately six inches apart.

The semi-wooded area we were fencing was about 100 yards long, so it took us a few days to complete the project.

During the first day, our officers saw the situation was stable. They lost interest by noon and left supervision to our more relaxed NCOs.

The next several days, as we worked, we tried to chat with the Russians and offered them cigarettes, but they muttered, "*Nyet*," and ignored our attempts.

Several of our crew had cars and drove them to the site.

On our breaks they would play AFN, Armed Forces Network, music on their car radios as we laid back and relaxed.

We could sense both envy and contempt from the Russians.

With the special project completed, we could return to our regular jobs. As we were packing up our tools and excess materials, one NCO commented to me, "Well, Schulist, now that your office guys had a chance to do some real work, what do you think of it?"

Before I could answer, one of the equipment operators said, "Sarge, I don't know if you noticed, but I did, Schulist outworked every man here." I smiled and said nothing. It was an exciting change for me, and I thoroughly enjoyed it.

Unexpected Encounter

In the late Fall of 1956, with Thanksgiving and Christmas coming near, the captain in charge of our Engineering Section operations arranged a holiday season party for the enlisted men of the Engineer Platoon. It was to take place at Club 48 which was the NCO Club. Dress was semi-formal with either dress civilian clothes or our dress uniforms. At the time, our dress uniforms were the style designed by Eisenhower with the famous, "Ike" jacket.

There would be drinks, dinner and music for dancing and socializing. Each G.I. could bring one guest.

My roommate Carmen said, "Lou, you have no one to take, why don't you come sit at a table with me and my German girlfriend." I accepted Carmen's invitation. At the NCO club I joined Carmen and met his girlfriend Irma. She was a pretty, pleasant, blonde.

Irma spoke a little English and I spoke enough German to converse a bit. Because I would be working with Germans, I was given the opportunity to attend an Army class for basic, conversational German. The class helped me greatly to slowly grow a vocabulary in German and, this evening, it helped me converse and get acquainted with Irma.

It was a nice evening. Our Captain and his charming wife visited each of our tables and chatted freely with all of us. Being enlisted men, we were impressed by their relaxed friendliness and their genuine interest in us. They asked about our backgrounds and our families back in the States. They had a group photo taken with each table and we each got a copy several days later.

The drinks were generous, the dinner was great, and the music was soft and romantic.

With Carmen's approval, I danced several dances with Irma. Each dance became a little warmer. I looked into her blue eyes and received a smile.

Throughout the evening, when I looked at Carmen's date, Irma, I noticed she seemed to be studying me closely.

At the end of the evening, as we were saying our goodbyes, Irma shyly asked me, "Lou, do you have a girlfriend?"

"No," I replied. "I lost my American girlfriend when I joined the Army."

Irma took my hand, looked at me, and said, "Lou, I have a girlfriend that I think you would like very much, and I think she would like you very much. Would you like to meet her?"

"Yes, I would like that," I said, not wanting to hurt Irma's feelings. I didn't know what might come of it.

The following week Carmen said, "Lou, I took Irma to a movie on Post. She told me she and her girlfriend would be at the Schloss Cafe Saturday evening around 6:00 pm. Do you want to go and meet them?"

I didn't want to go back on my word, so I said, "Yes."

Saturday mornings typically consisted of hands-on training on engineering heavy equipment or, company meetings and training lectures.

Usually, we were free after Saturday lunch.

Around 5:30, Carmen and I showered, dressed in our "civvies" and hopped the streetcar to my blind date.

The Schloss Cafe was a nice medium size bar with dance music. It was a favorite hangout of mostly Service Company G.I.'s. I believed it was where Carmen met his friend Irma months earlier before I arrived in Berlin.

Carmen and I sat at a table sipping our beers and watching the door.

I was about to go to the restroom to check in the mirror to see how I looked.

Just then Carmen said, "Lou, here comes Irma and she has her friend with her."

As they approached our table, I stood up and smiled. Irma smiled back and said, in German, "Lou, please meet Brigitte," then, "Brigitte, please meet Lou."

In German, Brigitte is pronounced with three syllables, *Bri-git-teh*. All the vowels have the "short" sound.

I thought, *what a pretty name*, as I looked at the young woman it belonged to.

Brigitte had lustrous, long brown hair and pleasant, brown eyes. She was modestly and nicely dressed.

She radiated a wholesome charm and I immediately felt she was special.

Brigitte reached out her hand to me, smiled, and said, "Hello."

As I took her hand, I noticed that her smile showed her pretty teeth. Brigitte was slim and nicely proportioned. I was five-feet-ten inches tall and guessed her to be about five-feet-six.

I invited Brigitte to please sit down and let me order her a drink.

As she sipped her mix of Coke and Brandy, I told her about my home and my family in Michigan.

I learned that Brigitte lived in the Berlin borough of Neukölln. She told me she worked as a seamstress for a woman who designed exclusive housecoats for women.

Brigitte asked me if I liked to dance. I took the hint and invited her to the dance floor.

She was light on her feet and gracefully and easily followed my lead. She danced warmly but modestly. As we danced, I noticed her beautiful, almost olive, complexion. When she spoke, her breath was sweet and fresh.

At our table, we chatted in a mixture of my basic German and her minimal school English.

Over the next several hours, we talked, had more drinks, and danced more dances.

I sensed that Brigitte's war experiences, being born and raised in Berlin, had given her a youthful maturity and an absence of frivolity.

We both became comfortably at ease with each other.

We seemed to forget Carmen and Irma were with us and we mostly left them to themselves. I realized it was getting late and Carmen and I had to be back on base by midnight, so, the time had come to say goodnight.

We all waited together at the streetcar stop for our streetcars which would be going in opposite directions.

As we waited, I asked Brigitte, "May I see you again?"

She smiled and said, "I would like that, but how? My family has no phone."

I also had no phone access. It was obvious we would need to immediately plan our next date.

I said, "If you take this streetcar to the end, it stops near the gate at Andrews Barracks. Can you come Wednesday and meet me at the gate at around 6:30? I will meet you, sign you in, and we can go to the movie on post."

Brigitte said, "I will try to be there."

As her and Irma's streetcar approached, I asked Brigitte, "May I kiss you goodnight."

She turned her face up to me. As I held her in my arms and kissed her goodnight, my heart quickened.

Carmen and I made the regular quick stop at the Bratwurst stand near the barracks front gate.

We got our bock-wurst, hard roll, and hot mustard orders wrapped in butcher paper and took them back to our room.

As we sat on our bunks, enjoying our late-night snacks Carmen asked, "Well, Lou, what do you think of Brigitte?"

"I think she's special," I said. "I like her, and I plan to see her again. I'm happy, Irma thought to introduce us."

Wednesday, I hurried through the mess hall dinner, then, changed from my work fatigues to my civvies.

At about 6:00, I was out the gate and over to the *Goldenen Sonne*. I nursed a beer and watched anxiously out the window for the next streetcar to arrive.

I was relieved when Brigitte arrived as planned.

She stepped from the streetcar and looked around. I left my beer and ran across the street to meet her.

She looked lovely and was again simply but nicely dressed. We held hands as I walked her to the gate. After I signed her in at the guardhouse, I felt proud of her as I walked with her across the parade ground to the service club theater.

As the theater darkened and the movie began, I put my arm around her and tried to draw her close to me. She smiled at me, took my arm from around her shoulders, and instead, held my hand.

After the movie, I invited her for a hamburger in the post service club snack bar.

She enjoyed the burger but was self-conscious trying to hold it together and eat it.

She said she felt like everyone was watching her. I said, "No, they're all busy with their own messy sandwiches."

As we had chatted in the snack bar, I learned that Brigitte rose at 6:00 am each weekday to get ready, walk the four blocks to a main street, and then catch a bus to her job as a seamstress.

She worked with three other women who, like her, worked at pattern cutting tables and sewing machines making designer housecoats for women. This took place in a large room in the home of the boss and owner, Frau Barkow, who designed the housecoats and ran the business.

I signed Brigitte out at the gate and waited with her, for the next streetcar to take her home.

I felt sorry for her when she told me she must take the streetcar to where it meets the elevated train, then, transfer and take the elevated train to the station near her home. Then, she must walk four blocks from the train station to home.

It was near Christmas and our next date was for a New Year's Eve party to take place in a large room several GIs had rented in a German widow woman's home.

I attended Christmas 1956 midnight Mass on post and, for the first time since I left home, I didn't feel alone.

On New Year's Eve, I met Brigitte at the Schloss Cafe.

Together, we found the address where the party was being held. We socialized with the other couples and several of the widow's friends and neighbors who were invited. The room had a balcony and at midnight, we looked out over the street where fireworks were being shot off.

Brigitte and I kissed and wished each other a happy new year.

We learned that the hostess widow had a daughter, named Waltraud, who had dated and eventually married a G.I. from the 6th Infantry regiment.

They would soon be leaving Berlin for his home in Texas.

Shortly after midnight, they came home and entered the party. Waltraud's Texan husband had obviously over-indulged and was in a surely mood. He spotted one of our group, Reuben, who was obviously Mexican.

Uttering profanities, he questioned Reuben's presence and was about to confront him. We quickly intervened and Waltraud coaxed him away and to bed. Waltraud re-entered the room and apologized. Reuben said, "Don't worry, I'm used to it, and, if you're going to live in Texas, you will get used to it too."

The unpleasant incident spoiled the mood and the celebration soon broke up. Also, our New Year's Eve passes, which were extended to 2:00 am, would soon expire.

It was obvious that finding time to be together wouldn't be easy. We would really have to want to see each other.

For the next weeks, our dates took place mostly on post for movies and snacks.

Sometimes, we would meet at German establishments which had food, drinks and, usually, music and dancing. Although I would occasionally spot a G.I. friend with his girlfriend and we would share a table with them, we were comfortable and happy just being alone and doing things together.

Brigitte always looked fresh and lovely and was always pleasant to be with. I could quickly single Brigitte out within any group and my heart always quickened and warmed seeing her.

In late Spring of 1957, a barracks friend, Bob, from St. Louis, urged me to accompany him on a leave, from Berlin, to visit Paris, London and Amsterdam. We would divide two weeks between the three destinations. I was reluctant because I didn't want to be away from my new girlfriend, Brigitte, that long. He argued, "Here we are in Europe with an opportunity to visit these three great cities very inexpensively because we're already here at Uncle Sam's expense! Distances aren't so great like in the US. We'll travel by trains and ferry boats." It was all true, so I agreed.

After listening to my exciting news, Brigitte said, "How nice, I hope you won't forget about me. I hope you will be good."

We got our leave orders issued along with the Russian translations to get us through East Germany. We went by the military train from Berlin to West Germany.

We continued by train, through Germany and France, and arrived in Paris. We found a small hotel where, fortunately, the proprietor and I could converse in German. Maybe he learned during the WWII occupation.

We found our way to the Champs Elysée despite an unhelpful cab driver. I told the driver several times, pronouncing the name of the famous street as best I could, where we wanted him to take us. He shrugged his shoulders and shook his head as though I were speaking Chinese to him. Bob found the name in the itinerary he had with him. He showed the driver the printed name. The driver brightened and said the name, not much differently than I had, and put the cab in gear. I learned that this aloofness was a typical French mannerism. I experienced it both there in France and then later in Quebec, Canada.

We visited all the famous attractions and were impressed. Paris had a fascinating air about it. As we walked along, we were obviously easily spotted as Americans. On two occasions we were approached by young Algerians.

They portrayed friendly helpful smiles and used understandable English. They were anxious to get American dollars and offered us attractive exchange rates for French Francs. We suspected a counterfeit scheme and gave them a friendly refusal. We told them we had all the Francs we would need. We then became extra cautious to stay on busy streets.

I learned later that the young men were probably anti-French Colonialism members of the Algerian National Liberation Front (FLN). They were fighting for freedom from French rule of their country.

They wanted the solid American dollars to more effectively finance their cause. American dollars were readily accepted currency internationally.

Their war was short but vicious. France later admitted that they had violated the Geneva Convention rules against prisoner torture. The Algerians prevailed and gained their independence.

From France we took the train to the English Channel.

We crossed the channel by boat and then boarded a coal burning steam train to London. The soot from the engine was evident in our compartment.

Sharing our compartment were two young and pretty ladies. Bob quickly struck up a conversation with them. They were Americans touring Europe, London was their next destination. We introduced ourselves and joked and chatted as young folks do. I excused myself to use the restroom. When I returned, I sensed a slight change in the relaxed atmosphere. We continued to visit, and we became comfortable enough with each other that we agreed to meet that evening around seven P.M. at the statue of Eros in Piccadilly Circus. We would than find a restaurant and have dinner together. We parted at the train depot.

Bob had the address of a low-cost rooming place that he had gotten from a barracks friend in the Headquarters company. The taxi delivered us to the Queens Hotel, Kingsbury Terrace.

It looked clean but spartan. It was a long attic room with six military style bunks. There were currently three of us there. We met the other guest, a U.S. airman stationed in the

London area. He was staying in the hotel because he was on a three-day pass and wanted to be away from military quarters for a change. We mentioned that we were anxious to visit an English Pub and try some ale. He told us that to enjoy the ambiance of a Pub you had to be a member. He told us joining a Pub was simple, but he was already a member of a Pub and he would enjoy bringing us in as guests. Bob said, "Let's go!" I said, "What about the two girls? We agreed we would meet them for a dinner date." Bob replied, "Forget them Lou, this will be a more interesting experience."

When I think of it, I still deeply regret giving in to Bob's decision. It's a despicable, cowardly thing for a man to not show up for a date and leave a woman standing. It's OK in my thinking if a woman doesn't show. A woman has much more at stake.

The Pub was interesting and the Ale from the long-handled pump was a new experience. We drank and watched the dart throwers. It was a "jolly time."

Back in our hotel, in the evening, we found a simple room service menu. Bob picked up the phone and in his best British imitation, ceremoniously ordered, "Tea for two please and two ham and cheese sandwiches on toast." I have never had a ham and cheese since, that could equal the flavor and robustness of that wonderful sandwich. Maybe I was just very hungry.

As we sat enjoying our repast, I mentioned to Bob that I sensed a change in the two girls on the train after I returned from the restroom.

Bob laughed, "Oh that, while you were away," I said quietly to them, 'don't say anything to Lou about what I'm quickly going to tell you.' Then I told them, 'Lou is an American agent who spies for us in the East. They want him to go on this trip to relieve the stress he works under. He doesn't know, but I've been sent along with orders to keep a close watch on him. He could be a double agent.'"

"I know Lou, and I'm sure he isn't, so don't worry."

That explained it. Bob had a good imagination and would make, and maybe was, a con man.

We stayed only the one night in London and didn't really see that great city's famous sights. Bob, planned our itinerary, based on the stories he heard from his friends who had made the same trip. They advised that we want to spend the most of our time in Amsterdam.

From the coast of England, we boarded a large boat headed for what, Bob said, was The Hook of Holland.

It was a several hour trip. We sat in deck chairs and relaxed. A young man walked over to a young lady sitting alone and began talking to her. She listened awhile then asked him, "Where are you from?"

"New Zealand," he replied.

She said, "I always wondered about your country, what does you flag look like?"

He replied with a leer, "You can best see it by dark. Let's you and I find a dark corner and I'll describe it to you."

She got up from her chair and told him, "Get lost!" She came over and sat in the attached chair next to me. I waited to see if he would follow her, but he walked away. I was relieved that he left.

She looked at me and said, "You're an American, I know what your flag looks like. It's beautiful."

She told me she is Dutch and returning to her home in the Hague section of the Netherlands. She had visited family friends in England. As we got out further over the water, the air got noticeably cooler. She reached to a pile of lap blankets beside her and selected a fresh looking one. She opened it, spread it over the two of us and snuggled up to me with a pretty smile.

As we neared land, she asked me where I was headed in Holland.

I told her my partner and I were going to Amsterdam.

She said, "Amsterdam is fun but why don't you let your friend go alone and you stay here in The Hague for a few days? You can stay with me and my parents. I can show you around and I'm sure we'd both enjoy it." *Oh my! The world never ceases to tempt us with alluring opportunities.* I thought of my Brigitte.

"I'm a soldier," I said, "My partner and I are traveling under the same orders which required us to disclose our itinerary. We're expected to follow it."

"I would love to accept your invitation and I'm sure I'll often wonder about what I missed." We wished each other well, kissed goodbye, and parted. I never told Brigitte that otherwise charming story.

Our stay in Amsterdam was in a barracks type room similar to our London hotel. This was on the second floor of a local family's home. We ate our included meals with the family members but were free to come and go as we pleased. There were two other male guests in the large room. Both were American military who, like us, were on leave enjoying as much of Europe as their leave time permitted.

The lifestyle of the Dutch in Amsterdam was far different from that of the Dutch I remembered in Muskegon, Michigan.

Uninhibited, individual freedom seemed to be the accepted and apparently happy norm. We partied with the locals and tourists, mostly in outdoor bistros. Each had an MC who saw to it that it was a group affair with everyone involved and enjoying the somewhat ribald fun.

Good Dutch beer and Schnapps kept everyone loose and jovial. Background music helped set the mood.

Our several days in Amsterdam went quickly. We took the canal tour in a comfortable boat and followed the canal to its meeting with the sea. I thought it would be interesting to watch the ice-skating traffic on the frozen canals in the winter.

The two weeks ended, and we found our way back, mostly by train, to Berlin and duty.

I had told Brigitte that I would meet her at the Schloss Café on my first Saturday back. I sat down, ordered a beer and waited. She soon arrived and came to my table. I stood up and hugged her. It seemed so good to be with her again. We sat down and the waiter came. I ordered Brigitte her Coke and Brandy and myself another beer. She wanted to know about my adventures. I gave her the tourist watered down version leaving out some details. She said, "I want to tell you something. I went out dancing in East Berlin with Irma one Saturday while you were gone. I hope you're not mad." I thought it was mild compared to my happenings.

I said, "No I'm not mad and I'm glad that you were honest and told me. You didn't need to."

Several months of dating had gone by when, one warm evening, I went out the gate to meet Brigitte for our evening's date.

Instead, I found Brigitte's friend, Irma, waiting for me.

Irma motioned me over to her and said, "Lou, I have some bad news for you. Brigitte asked me to come and meet you and to tell you she didn't really care for you and didn't want to see you anymore."

Irma continued on, "Lou, I don't want you to be sad so I will be happy to be your girlfriend. I will be good to you. You can forget about Brigitte and be happy with me."

I couldn't believe what I was hearing.

I said, "Irma, I thank you for your offer to be my girlfriend but, I really care for Brigitte. If she really doesn't care for me, I need to hear that from her."

Irma burst into tears. She turned and ran to board the streetcar which was about to leave. I went back to the barracks and sat on my bunk to think things over.

I didn't say anything to Carmen, who was getting ready to go out for the evening. We had stopped double-dating and I sensed he was no longer interested in Irma.

Carmen said, "See you later," and left.

A short while later, Carmen stuck his head back in the room. "Lou," he said. "I just went out the gate and saw Brigitte waiting out there. She called me over and asked me to please tell you she is waiting for you."

"Thanks, Carmen," I said. "Please hurry back out and tell her I'm on my way." I quickly straightened myself out and headed for the gate.

Brigitte was standing there looking as lovely as ever. She had a serious expression, and her first words were, "Is it true what Irma told me, that you asked her to tell me that you don't care for me and don't want to see me anymore?" Her eyes glistened with the beginning of tears.

I took her tightly into my arms and said, "Brigitte, you must know that's not true. Irma was here when I came out earlier to meet you. She told me you sent her to tell me you didn't care to see me anymore. Irma offered to be my girlfriend. I told Irma, 'No, if Brigitte no longer cares for me, I need to hear it from her.' Irma went away crying and left on the streetcar."

Brigitte thought for a moment and shook her head sadly.

It was a nice evening, so we held hands and walked toward a nearby park.

We were quiet except for admiring the flowers blooming along the way.

As we were about to enter the park, a Mercedes taxi pulled to the curb and a voice shouted out, "Hey Lou."

It was a barracks buddy, George, from Queens, New York. George was the one classmate from Fort Belvoir that I stayed in contact with. George also got assigned to Berlin and was several rooms away in my barracks.

George and his girlfriend, Renate, were headed for a little neighborhood supper club type bar they had recently discovered. We were invited to join them.

We squeezed into the taxi. Brigitte and Renate chatted and became acquainted as we drove along.

The bar, named, *The Insel Bar*, was cozy. The background music was soft, and the drinks were good and nicely served. There was no dancing going on, so we sat and chatted. Brigitte and I sat on an upholstered bench facing

George and Renate, who were in chairs across the table from us.

The evening went on and, with the drinks and the soft music, the mood became mellow.

A large old dog came and plumped itself down on the floor behind my and Brigitte's bench. It was probably the proprietor's dog, and this was obviously the dog's place to stretch out and relax.

The dog's relaxed breathing added to the coziness of the moment.

George and Renate were now in what appeared to be a close personal conversation so, Brigitte half turned and began to pet the old dog behind us. I turned and joined her and again I saw tears glistening in her eyes. "Lou, there is something I must tell you, maybe now is the time. Maybe, after you hear me, you will want to have Irma as your girlfriend."

I looked at Brigitte and waited.

"I have a two-year-old son," she said, "His name is Jack. That's why I haven't invited you to my home to meet my family." She took her hand away from petting the dog and squeezed my arm.

She looked closely at me and, in her broken English, pleadingly said, "Please don't mad at me, please don't mad at me."

I was at a loss for words and, for a minute, sat quietly.

"Do you love Jack's father?" I finally asked.

She said, "Yes, I did love him, we were going to be married, but he's gone."

"Forever?" I asked.

"Yes, forever," she replied.

118

I didn't need or want to know any more details and I never asked or mentioned it again. Coming from a large family of brothers, sisters, uncles, aunts, and many cousins, I had learned we are all human and life can quickly become complicated. I understood. I wasn't angry. I had come to sense and to respect Brigitte's basic qualities of goodness. Besides, I had made no serious commitments to her, except perhaps in my heart.

I put an arm around Brigitte and asked if I could meet her family and her son.

Brigitte looked at me and said, "Lou I told my mother about you. I asked her if I could start having you visit me in our home. My mother said, 'Invite him here for a Sunday visit so I can meet him, then, we will see.'" Brigitte asked me, "Will you come and visit."

"Yes, I would like that very much," I replied.

She was relieved at my reaction and pleased that I wanted to meet her family.

After we parted from George and Renate, Brigitte gave me her address and invited me for a visit the coming Sunday.

"Are you angry at Irma?" I asked.

"No," she replied.

"Irma has always been a close friend. I feel sorry for her because she loves you and can't have you, because I hope you will stay with me. Also," she said, "Irma brought us together."

We left the Insel Bar and walked along the cobblestone sidewalk holding hands. Because we came with George and Renate's taxi, we weren't sure where we were. To be safe, we hailed a passing taxi and had the driver take us to

Schloss Strasse. There, we were familiar with the area and could each catch our familiar streetcars.

Back in the barracks, I lay awake for a long time turning the dramatic events of the day over in my mind. I wasn't worried, but I wondered what the future now held for me in my new relationship, far away from my home and family.

Sunday morning, I went to Mass at the Andrews Barracks chapel. I prayed for guidance and wisdom to both know and do the right thing in my relationship with Brigitte.

After Mass, I went back to my room and selected my most appropriate civilian clothes.

I felt a nervous sense of anticipation at this new development in my life in Berlin.

My journey to the Neukölln area was new to me; although I learned later that it was near Tempelhof airfield where my co-workers, I, and our assigned driver, frequently had our between appointment coffee breaks.

I rode quite a distance on the streetcar watching ahead for the bridge over the roadway which would indicate the elevated train intersection.

At the elevated train station, I paid the fare and climbed the steps to the platform. I checked to make sure I would get the train going the right direction to take me to my exit station. It was about a twenty-minute-high-speed ride, with several station stops along the way. Riders got off and on quickly under the watchful eye of a station master who would blow a sharp high-pitched whistle to signal the train to proceed.

As I got off the elevated train, and walked from the station, I discovered I was right at the intersection with Brigitte's home street. I walked the four blocks of cobblestone sidewalks watching for her house number. I now realized how much travel effort it took for Brigitte to come to meet me for our dates. The rows of four-story apartment buildings looked alike with balconies on each level.

I found the apartment building and, because it was still early evening, the main entrance door was unlocked.

I climbed the stairs to her families third floor apartment and knocked on the door. Along the way, I noticed several apartment doors that were slightly ajar. They closed quietly after I passed by. Brigitte's mom must have told her widowed neighbor friends that an *"Ami"* was coming to visit her Brigitte. They were curious to get a peek at me.

A young man, looking several years older than myself, answered the door with a curt, "Yah?"

I looked him directly in the eyes and in my best basic German I said, "I am here to visit Brigitte."

He turned, shouted, "Brigitte," and disappeared down the hallway into a room.

Brigitte was expecting me and likely spotted me from their balcony but her older brother, Herbert, probably insisted on first sizing me up at the door.

I learned later that Herbert, his wife Gertrud, and their toddler son Reinhard were immigrating to Toronto, Canada and would leave the very next day.

Brigitte came to the door and, blushing slightly, took me into the kitchen to meet her mother, Elfriede.

I immediately realized that I should have brought some flowers along for my first visit. Too late.

Elfriede smiled graciously and welcomed me. She offered me a coffee and we sat and chatted for a short while. She spoke no English, so conversation of any depth wasn't possible.

Brigitte then led me into a large room, which I learned, served as a living room, dining room, and, as a bedroom for Brigitte, her younger half-sister Renate and her younger brother, Gunter.

Furniture was sparse but functional and consisted of a large dining table with chairs, a sofa, a large standing closet for hanging and storing clothes, a cot for Gunter in the corner near the door and a large double bed near a tall double window.

In one corner of the room, stood a large, ceramic stove which burned coal bricks and radiated heat for the room and the adjacent hall area. There were double glass doors which opened to the balcony. All was neat and tidy. Brigitte introduced me to Gunter and Reni. Then she said, "Here's my son, Jack." He was an attractive child.

I spent my first visit answering questions from Reni and Gunter and getting acquainted with the bright toddler, Jack, who was soon sitting on my knee.

Brigitte graciously tried to make me feel as much at ease as possible in this new situation. I was fine. I felt comfortable and ready to let things evolve in this new direction my life was taking.

I wasn't yet familiar enough with my travel time and connections so, I left at 10:00 pm to make sure I'd be back through the Andrews Barrack gate before midnight. Brigitte walked me down to the main entrance door. We planned our next date. She thanked me for my visit, kissed me good night and gave me the standard German departure wish, "*Komm gute nach haus.*"—Come home good.

It was obvious that the easiest way for us to spend time together was for me to come to Brigitte's home.

With no responsibilities but myself, I could quickly leave the barracks after supper and have about four hours to spend visiting before catching the elevated train for the trip back to the barracks. We continued to meet for movie dates and, Brigitte became my guest for the captain's occasional platoon parties at the NCO club.

Brigitte's mom encouraged her to, "Have Lou visit you here at home." It was less hectic, and Elfriede probably liked the freedom from the frequent baby-sitting.

On those evenings, when I visited, we typically went for a walk around the neighborhood or sat in the living room and listened to music. Herbert left his record player and his record collection, and I bought some American records to play. I also brought a small Telefunken radio. Brigitte liked Elvis. She also liked listening to *Gun Smoke* on the Radio in the American Sector.

During the ensuing months, I became integrated into Brigitte's Berlin family. Birthdays always meant a gathering of most relatives including some from the East Zone. They were uncles, aunts and cousins.

Fridays and Saturdays frequently meant a small house gathering, often at Brigitte's older sister Ellie's home several doors away.

Ellie was married to Werner who worked as a conductor on the Subway. They had two young sons, Dieter and Detlef. Werner had been a member of a German panzer crew on the Russian front. When Germany's eastern front collapsed, Werner became a Russian POW for a short while. His war experiences affected his personality. Werner could be charming, friendly and humorous but was prone to jealousy and anger and would frequently strike Ellie.

The two young boys would relate the abuse incidents to the rest of the family. Brigitte and others urged Ellie to take her two sons and flee to West Germany.

Ellie was afraid to leave Werner. Maybe, knowing his combat background, she still loved him and excused his outbursts of abuse.

The bloody fighting and horror of intense combat on the Russian front had left its mark on body and soul.

Many who fought there were physically and mentally scarred.

Brigitte told me that her older brother, Herbert, was somewhat of a threat to Werner and had frequently warned Werner not to mistreat their sister, Ellie.

But Herbert was now living in Canada and the protective umbrella he provided was gone.

Often, friends of Ellie and Werner joined the gatherings.

Typically, we all sat around a large table with a brandy glass in front of each of us. A large bottle of Deutsche Weinbrand, German Brandy, sat in the middle of the table. Occasionally, as the evening wore on, someone would notice that the glasses had become empty and would pour another round. The sipping continued and the conversation became livelier. My presence helped my German to improve and to better reflect local jargon and pronunciation.

Also, I learned that German conversation was much more direct and less diplomatic than our typical American way. After conversations with some of our British allies, I concluded that directness may be a European trait in general. I guessed that by living through a vicious war Europeans learned not to waste words.

The conversations of Brigitte's family were mostly about daily life and often went over my head.

They could tell by my expression when I was lost, and they would usually slow down and bring me back. The gatherings tended more toward humor and good times and seldom dwelt on serious matters. I think it was helpful for me that most surviving Berlin males had fought Russians, not Americans. Now, as allies, we were comfortable with each other. Also, it seemed soldiers understood soldiers.

Sundays, I was free for the entire day and, after Sunday Mass on base, I would head for Brigitte's home.

On several occasions, I attended Mass at a German church near Brigitte's home. Because Catholic Mass was universally in Latin during those times, I felt right at home. I somewhat understood the homilies in German.

I was surprised at how sparsely attended the Sunday service was. Perhaps the Lutherans did better.

Religion, which was stifled under Hitler, was apparently still struggling to re-affirm itself in Germany.

Brigitte's mom began to plan on my presence and would have a plate for me for the Sunday mid-day meal. She was a good cook and the usual wiener schnitzel, mashed potatoes, gravy, vegetables, and a thick slice of dark bread with unsalted butter were always delicious. I began to look forward to it. Our mess hall food was good, but Elfriede's home cooking was better.

I learned that earlier, Elfriede worked as a cook at a popular local restaurant. She was able to quit and stay home with her family when she began to receive her war widow's benefits.

On nice days, we would go for an outing in one of the large, well-kept parks or wooded areas.

Brigitte would bring a blanket, and we would lie back, relax, and watch Jack run and play. We had bonded as a little family and enjoyed doing simple things together.

Jack was at ease with me and liked me to hold him and have him sit on my lap.

Later, we would walk to a bakery and buy a large piece of apple strudel and a paper tray of whipped cream.

At home, Brigitte would brew us coffee made from fresh ground coffee beans. Her mom would buy green coffee beans, roast them herself, and then the family would grind them in a little grinder as needed. The ground coffee was measured into the ceramic coffee pot and boiling water was poured on them. It was allowed to sit for a while. Each cup was then poured through a wire strainer. It was exceptionally good coffee and with the apple strudel and whipped cream was a nice Sunday afternoon treat.

This was usually followed by soft music and a quiet, relaxing nap.

The Cold War continued and, in 1956, had become more tense with the Hungarian's uprising against Russia's restrictive control. Any political activity in the Eastern

European countries caused uneasiness and reaction in East Germany and Berlin.

There were sporadic demonstrations in East Berlin and the surrounding East Germany. The Stars and Stripes military newspaper reported that the Russians had ringed Berlin with tanks and armored troop reinforcements.

The Berlin Allies began having joint readiness alerts.

On such alerts, I was assigned to requisition a two-and-a-half-ton truck from the motor pool. I was instructed to load the truck with several cases of rations and to "simulate" loading on "hasty fortifications" in the form of concertina wire. Because it was a practice alert, we wouldn't load the wire. I and one accompanying soldier would then drive to the British Sector and link up with a small token group of British soldiers who would be waiting for us. The plan was that in the event of a real Russian invasion of our sectors we "Yanks" would provide the materials and join the "Brits" to set up lines of defense.

The true value of the alerts was to show the Russians that the Western allies were prepared and determined to defend their Berlin sectors. The Western Allies activities in Berlin were always closely watched by the Russians.

After exchanging greetings and friendly barbs with the Brits, we would all get to the serious business of ripping open the C/K rations to salvage anything appealing.

We looked for such items as the four-packs of somewhat stale cigarettes, chocolate, and some of the tastier ready to eat meals. Cold scrambled eggs and ham weren't too bad and were the favorite.

We were not expected to return the cases of rations and we never did. The unwanted remnants went into a scrap barrel which the Brits provided.

The Brits also had one barrel, with a cheerful fire going, which we stood around while we smoked, chatted and waited for the "all clear" to be declared.

Recently, the Egyptians had nationalized the Suez Canal. This was a vital waterway to the British.

Britain responded by dropping British airborne troops, into Egypt, along the canal. They were there to protect Great Britain's interests and their ship movements passing through the Suez Canal.

The US had joined other UN members in denouncing Britain's invasion of a sovereign country.

As we stood by the barrel fire, one Brit looked at me and said, "Hey, Yank, why did you Yanks denounce our actions in Egypt, at the UN? I thought we were close partners who stuck together." He looked at me expectantly, awaiting my answer.

I smiled at him and said, "We are partners. I'm sure that before Britain made the move into Egypt, London contacted Washington and said, 'We've made the decision to seize the Suez Canal. We know we're breaking international law by doing it, but we need to protect our vital interests.'

"I'm sure the US replied, 'You know that we will need to take a strong public stand against you to support international law but, we understand completely, and we wish you success.'"

Then, I said in a complementary tone, "You Brits got it done in your typical crisp and efficient way."

Another Brit, standing there listening, exclaimed, "The Yank is right, E's bloody brilliant!"

I wasn't sure if I was right, but I felt it should have been that way and probably was. Eventually, the alert was terminated. We said goodbye to the Brits and returned to the American Sector and the Andrew Barracks compound.

In Cold War Berlin, I felt reassured and grateful that our trusted allies France and especially Great Britain joined us in our commitment to defend West Berlin.

The value of cooperation with our close allies cannot be overstated and, must always be protected and nurtured. We are strongest when we strive first for the shared common good, keeping in mind our individual national interests. All allies must be willing to compromise.

Things remained tense during the Hungarian uprising. For approximately a week, the Hungarians were gaining control of Budapest.

Leaders of the uprising were beginning to emerge and assert themselves. For years, America's Radio Free Europe had been broadcasting to the Eastern bloc countries, urging them to resist Communism and take a stand for free elections and democracy. Now that Hungary had taken bold steps against Russian control, they were looking to America for material, and hopefully, military support. There were reports that they were on their roof tops watching for American airborne support to arrive.

President Eisenhower reluctantly made the decision not to intervene and risk war with Russia.

The Hungarians felt that the USA had deceived and deserted them. America would not intervene with support.

Seeing their way clear, the Russians quickly moved in tanks and troops to quell the uprising.

The leaders of the unsuccessful effort were arrested, and some were executed. Many Hungarians, fearing retaliation, fled to the West. Some made their way to the US.

The world condemned Russia's vicious assault on Hungary, but Russia countered by claiming it was no worse than Britain's assault on Egypt's Suez Canal.

In the Berlin area, the Russians dropped propaganda leaflets showing a husky British soldier sitting on top of a fallen, little, Egyptian wearing his little fez hat. In the background were the canal and a pyramid.

The British soldier was reading a newspaper and, in the caption, was exclaiming, "Oh those poor Hungarians!"

In Berlin, and East Germany, the Cold War tension relaxed a little but still went on.

The bustling and prosperous West Berlin economy far outshone the surrounding drab and struggling East German economy and austere way of life. Khrushchev wanted desperately to get the Western Allies out of Berlin. He stated, "West Berlin is like a bone in my throat."

The existence of Cold War espionage was evident to some degree in our Engineering Clearance Section work.

We frequently went through the process of providing civilian type housing for "spook" groups. This included not only housing for our own operatives, but also for personnel from Eastern Bloc countries who were allegedly spying for the West.

The several eastern European bloc agents I dealt with were friendly but cautious. They were insistent that we begin our session with a "toast" with Vodka or Slivovitz.

They also wanted to carefully review and understand everything I wrote in my report.

On the several "moving out" inspections I made, they requested that I report no discrepancies or damages. They said, "Just point them out and we will get them fixed ourselves." Fortunately, I found none so we didn't have to hassle that out.

Berlin was a main jumping off point for spies entering or leaving Eastern Europe. Kidnappings and killings of operatives, by both sides, sometimes occurred and were occasionally reported in the Berlin newspapers.

Eventually, exchanges of several high visibility persons would be negotiated and would take place cautiously on the Glienicke Bridge, which was located on the dividing line between West Berlin and East Germany.

The bridge was over a span of water and conveniently provided clear and open vision of activities occurring on each side's approach to the prisoner exchange line.

Although I visited Brigitte regularly, I was required to be back in the barracks by midnight. I typically returned to my room shortly before midnight when most GIs were already asleep, and the barracks were quiet.

One night was an exception. As I was climbing the stairs, I heard a high-pitched cry of panic. Someone was in distress and crying, "Stop it! Leave me alone!"

As I topped the stairs, I saw one of our NCOs, a Corporal Briar, slapping around a recently arrived Private Simms. Simms was offering no resistance and was trying to protect himself with his upheld hands. It was the Private's cries I had heard. The hall was otherwise empty. Simms was in his underwear shorts and was apparently accosted as he was heading for the restroom.

Briar had a tough guy reputation. He spoke in a rasping voice., worn out from whiskey. He bragged often of having boxed as a professional. When Briar saw me top the stairs, he stopped his attack, went down the hall to the NCO section, and entered his room. He appeared unsteady. I continued to my room wondering what would have happened to Simms if I hadn't happened to come upon the scene. Though I certainly didn't consider myself an angel, I wondered, *Was I Simms's "guardian angel," appearing at just the right time?*

I've observed over the years that helping and rescuing angels do occasionally appear, in various forms, and usually aren't recognized as such until maybe long after.

I particularly recall an instance when my faithful 1985 Chevy pickup stalled at a stoplight at a busy intersection. It was rush hour and traffic was heavy in all directions. I sat cranking the engine as I heard the horns impatiently honking behind me. I put my emergency flashers on and looked for my cell phone. Suddenly, there was a knock at my window. I rolled it down. A young lady, covered with tattoos, said, "We got to get you out of this busy spot before someone gets hurt or killed. I'm going to stop traffic behind you and get a couple of volunteers to push you over to that gas station parking area." Within minutes, it was done. I was safe and traffic again flowed.

I looked around, the young, tattooed lady and the several random volunteers had all jumped back in their cars and were gone. She saw the situation, took charge, made it happen and then, disappeared without my even having a chance to thank her. She was one of several strangers who over the years, "saved my butt." It also gave me a lesson in judging others too quickly by their appearance.

Early the next morning, before our morning outdoor assembly in ranks, the NCO on duty in the Orderly Room caught me in the hall. "Schulist," he said, "Last night Private Simms reported that he had been, for no reason, slapped around in the hall by Cpl. Briar. He gave your name as a witness."

I nodded, in affirmation.

He continued, "If questioned about the incident, what will you say?"

"I will tell the truth," I answered.

The NCO said no more and left.

After outdoor assembly and mess hall breakfast I was stopped in the hall by Private Simms.

He said, "I was told to let you know that Cpl. Briar has apologized to me. He admitted he was drunk and slapped me around without reason. He asked me to drop the charges and I did."

Then Simms told me, "Thank you for admitting you were a witness."

Nothing more was heard of it and, thankfully, Cpl. Briar continued to relate to me as casually as he always had.

Although NCOs had ways they could retaliate and make life difficult, in my forty-two months of active duty I didn't personally see that power abused.

Brigitte introduced me to a close friend, Regina. I was impressed by Regina's evident mental sharpness. She spoke English well and portrayed great self-confidence.

I was surprised to learn Regina was dating an American.

I was even more surprised when I met him.

Charlie was from Detroit and was stationed in Berlin with Military Intelligence. I learned, from him, that he did surveillance assignments. He drove an old, four-door Plymouth sedan that I assumed was provided for his work.

He also used it to date Regina. I rode in it several times when we double-dated.

Charlie was slight of build and very nondescript and ordinary appearing which was probably a plus for his covert type of work.

Charlie and Regina eventually did marry. Brigitte and I attended their Berlin wedding which became somewhat heated when Regina noticed Charlie admiring her older sister's ample bosom.

Charlie and Regina soon left for the US. Regina wrote to Brigitte. We learned later that they had a son but, sadly, divorced. Regina remained in the US and eventually re-married. She worked as a waitress in the Washington DC area where she met and married a Virginia State Trooper. Regina stopped writing eventually and we lost track of her. Brigitte said it no longer mattered.

My two roommates, Carmen and Bill, completed their tours of duty in close succession and were sent back to the States for discharge. There were no immediate replacement arrivals so, I had the barracks room to myself.

My across the hall friend, George, had married his girlfriend Renate and they would soon be leaving for life in Queens, New York.

This all made me begin to think of my own remaining time in Berlin and, of my future, regarding Brigitte.

I asked George if he and Renate would again like to go to the Insel Bar with Brigitte and me for an evening date.

George was willing so we arranged to meet there.

At the Insel Bar, I saw that the table with the bench under which the owner's old dog rested, was available, so I requested it. The four of us chatted, danced some, and enjoyed our mixed drinks. It was another charming and cozy evening with soft music. Later in the evening, George and Renate said their goodbyes and left us.

As we sat alone, listening to the music, I took Brigitte's hand and said, "You know I must soon leave Berlin and go back home to Michigan."

"I knew that must happen someday," she answered.

"I've thought about it a lot," I said. "I don't want to leave without you." She looked intently at me.

"Brigitte," I said, "I know that I love you, and, if you are willing, I want to marry you and take you and little Jack back to Michigan to begin our lives together there. Will you please marry me and go with me?"

Brigitte answered, "Lou, I know that I love you too. I was praying that you would ask me to marry you. Yes, Lou, I will marry you and go with you and live with you in America. I know you will take good care of us and I will help you all that I can." The evening took on a special meaning.

The next day, I woke up realizing I must begin whatever steps were needed to marry a German girl, adopt her son and take them with me to the USA.

I began by telling my decision to the First Sergeant. His first question was, "How long have you known this woman?" and, "Are you sure?" I told him I dated her for almost a year and a half and, yes, I was sure.

He told me I must talk to the company commander. He checked the captain's availability and sent me in to him.

After hearing my intentions and my request for clearance for marriage, the captain pulled my service record from his files. He looked it over and said, "I'm sorry, but you don't have enough time left in Berlin to complete all of the necessary paperwork."

"Sir, I'm certain of this," I said. "I am going to marry her. Can you discharge me here in Berlin?"

"No," he said. "But I have an idea. Let me check on it and I'll get back to you." I thanked him, saluted, and left.

The next morning, I was summoned to the Orderly Room.

"The Captain wants to see you," I was told.

"Specialist Schulist," the captain said, "If you are willing, I can extend your enlistment six months and keep you here in Berlin. Are you willing?"

"Yes, sir," I answered.

"Consider it done," he said. "See the first sergeant to get your necessary paperwork started."

This was early September1958. I now had six months to complete the paperwork and get married. I also had to plan to get Brigitte and Jack to Michigan.

I told Brigitte I had permission to proceed. I would be kept in Berlin six more months to allow the necessary time to complete the process and get married.

I took her to a jewelry store and bought her an adequate engagement ring. She was careful to pick one with several recessed small diamonds. She said that anything protruding out could snag on the material she worked with as a seamstress. The ring was more symbolic than showy, but Brigitte was pleased and happy, and so was I.

Several days after I had given Brigitte the ring, she told me that her mother had said, "Tell Lou that if he ever has overnight passes, he may stay with you. I will take Renate in my room with me."

I said to Brigitte, teasingly, "Would you like that."

She blushed, then, threw her arms around me and said, "Yes I think that would be very nice because I love you and we will soon be married."

My friend George, who had married his Renate, referred me to the German lawyer he had used for his marriage paperwork. He recommended him highly, both for his legal skill and his reasonable fee.

I first went alone to the address George gave me and knocked on the door. An elderly gentleman opened the door, looked at me and said, in English, "You are American, please come in, how can I help you?" I entered his small, but interesting home cluttered with books and knick-knacks. He invited me to sit down. I said, "I understand that you are a lawyer." He nodded. I explained that my friend George had recommended him and that I, like George needed legal help with marriage papers. I added that I also needed help with adoption paperwork. I gave him a quick summary of the relationship of Brigitte, Jack, and me.

He asked if I had cleared my intent with my commanding officer. I told him that I had approval and that I had been granted a six-month extension of my stay in Berlin to allow the necessary time.

Herr Goldschmidt said he would become my lawyer and help me through the legal process. He explained his fee and itemized and documented expenses contract.

I agreed to it. I knew that if anything went wrong, I would have access to Berlin Command's legal officer.

An evening appointment date was set for Brigitte and me to meet with our new lawyer.

Brigitte and I met with Herr Goldschmidt. He was a very charming Jewish lawyer who had somehow survived the Nazi's. Herr Goldschmidt chatted extensively with us using an effective mixture of German and English. He obviously wanted to assure himself that both Brigitte and I knew and understood what we were undertaking. He was almost fatherly in his approach. He explained to Brigitte all the legal records he would need access to from the German government.

Brigitte signed a paper authorizing him to have access to all her legal records.

Herr Goldschmidt not only flawlessly completed stacks of legal forms for the US and German governments but also compiled Brigitte's necessary documents from both East and West Berlin sources. He completed the adoption papers and acquired the necessary travel documents.

All paperwork, both the German and English translations, when submitted, were accepted without question.

Herr Goldschmidt was pleasant and friendly to work with and his price was embarrassingly low, 300 German Marks. At the 4.2 Marks to the dollar exchange rate at that time, it was 71 U.S. dollars.

I don't remember if Goldschmidt billed us for any expenses, but if he did, it was minimal.

When all preliminary paperwork was done, we both had to go to the U.S. Army hospital for blood tests.

Brigitte's blood drawing went fine. The jovial nurse then stuck the needle of a large syringe in my vein.

She drew out a large quantity of blood and, as I held a wad of gauze on the puncture wound, she squirted it into a test tube. She hadn't noticed but the very bottom of the receiving tube had broken off and was missing. My blood pooled on the smooth countertop.

The nurse saw my look of concern, expecting another needle insertion. To my amazement, using the syringe.
as a vacuum device, she sucked up, from the countertop, what she apparently thought was enough blood to complete my test. It must have been ok because we were both medically cleared for marriage.

The German Youth Protective Office certified Jack's good health.

Herr Goldschmidt told us all was in order. We could schedule our wedding day.

Brigitte and I bought a pair of engraved gold wedding bands at a jeweler near her home.

We had two small ceremonies, civil and religious.

Present were Brigitte, me, my best man, Brigitte's sister Ellie, and Brigitte's Mom.

First, we attended the civil function at the area clerk's office. We answered the required questions, said the right words and received our stamped and certified marriage papers.

We then proceeded to Andrews Barracks where a German priest, who volunteered to serve the Americans as a Chaplain, was waiting for us at the post chapel.

He was to perform a Catholic mixed marriage ceremony for us because Brigitte was a baptized and confirmed, although non-practicing, Lutheran.

We chatted a bit with the Chaplain before we began.

He asked Brigitte where she lived in Berlin. "I live in Berlin, Neukölln near Hermanstrasse," she replied.

The priest smiled and said, "Well, Brigitte, if you were Catholic, you would belong to my resident Parish which is in your neighborhood."

He proceeded with the ceremony. When the time came for me to put the ring on Brigitte's finger, it slipped from my hand and fell. I quickly snatched it up.

The priest smiled and said, "You caught it on the first bounce, that's a very good omen." I prayed that it was.

We were now married before God and man. It was Saturday December 6th, 1958.

Our modest wedding reception was held in Brigitte's family home. All of Brigitte's relations and friends were there including relatives from several East German cities. I had invited several of my closer and hopefully better-behaved barracks friends.

I had arranged to get four whole-dressed chickens from the main PX butcher shop. I had to time it carefully because there was no cooler or refrigeration available once I left the PX.

Brigitte's mom and several of her widow neighbor friends were busy putting together a wedding meal and were happy to receive the fresh chickens.

We had several cases of beer and several large bottles of German brandy. My army buddies mixed well with Brigitte's family, friends, and neighbors. We were all in the spirit of celebration. It was a wonderful party.

I had written a long letter to my parents telling them of my marriage details and my new son Jack. Although I had sent them pictures of Brigitte, I had never mentioned the possibility of marriage. They answered my letter as I expected, "We're looking forward to greeting you and your family. Your room will be ready when you get here."

Daily duty and barracks life continued.

We learned that General Anthony McAuliffe, of WWII Battle of the Bulge fame, was coming to Berlin.

McAuliffe was the American General who, when the German commander of the enemy surrounding the Americans sent a message demanding surrender, scrawled the word *NUTS* on the demand and sent it back.

McAuliffe's troops continued to hold off the Germans surrounding them in the Ardennes forest until one of General Patton's armored divisions fought their way to them and rescued them.

General McAuliffe would be reviewing Berlin operations. We were instructed that we would be standing in ranks for inspection wearing dress uniforms and, with our weapons.

I was excited that I would be personally seeing this famous General. I made sure my uniform and weapon were in impeccable shape.

General McAuliffe walked slowly but steadily through the ranks of soldiers standing at attention.

As he approached me, he paused in front of me. I did the mandatory act of coming to present arms. The General, looked at me and remarked, "This man presents himself very well," and then continued along the line of troops.

When the inspection was concluded, we were dismissed to return to our barracks.

In the barracks, I lay down on my bunk to rest and listen to my favorite Saturday afternoon radio program.

It was the Armed Forces Network's, *Here's to Veterans*. It was a music program featuring The Singing Sergeant's and, tastefully selected, restful music.

Often, as I listened, I drifted off into delicious episodes of being half asleep and half-awake enjoying the beautiful music.

This day I was interrupted with a message to report to the orderly room. As I entered, the First Sergeant was sitting at his desk. He smiled and said, "Good news, Schulist, you have a three-day pass."

I was confused and said, "It must be a mistake, I didn't put in a request for a three-day pass."

"No mistake," he said. "Our company commander was standing by and heard you get complimented by General McAuliffe at today's inspection."

The captain said, "It is quite an honor to be complemented by that great general and it deserves recognition. He ordered that you be given a three-day pass."

In later years, I heard of Napoleon complimenting a captive Russian artillery major for his bravery. The enemy major replied, "The greatest honor a soldier can receive is to be complimented by a great general."

I still cherish that simple honor.

The Sergeant already had the pass made out and he handed it to me. I hurried to my room and quickly got into my civvies and grabbed my shaving kit.

General McAuliffe didn't know it, but he had set me up for Brigitte's and my delayed marriage "honeymoon."

For three days and two nights, we were completely alone.

Brigitte and I spent the three days at a modest hotel on the Kurfurstendamm, Berlin's equivalent to New York's Broadway or maybe Fifth Avenue.

We strolled the sidewalks and even spent one evening at the Resi Bar. The Resi Bar was a classy, expensive place frequented mostly by doctors, lawyers, and businesspeople. It was famous for its table-to-table telephones and its spectacular musical, color-lighted, water fountain.

With the confidence that apparently comes with the wedding ring, Brigitte was becoming a bit more assertive.

I noticed that she relied a little less on my lead and was slowly beginning to make her own wishes and ideas more openly known.

I realized much later that it was the beginning of God's biblical "Two Becoming One" phenomenon which naturally occurs when there is blossoming love and mutual respect.

Given a chance, the "one" slowly grows and nurtures with time, love, and shared good and bad experiences.

Sadly, "Oneness" is easily taken for granted over the years but, it's always there, regardless.

Now married, I still had three months of duty in Berlin.

The First Sargent was lenient and allowed me an overnight pass when next day's work allowed it. I also typically had weekend passes.

We had good times relaxing, strolling the area and enjoying family gatherings. I shared Brigitte's half of the big double bed. Reni would go sleep with her mother.

When Brigitte knew I would stay, she would often stop at the nearby, dark and musky smelling wine cellar and get a bottle of Rhine wine for us to share. In the night, when I would awaken thirsty, she would always have a liter bottle of coke cooling on the windowsill. There was no refrigerator. Most food was bought fresh, almost daily, at the various, appropriate, neighborhood shops.

February of 1959 arrived and preparations for our journey to America began in earnest. My friendly relationship with the German office staff at the engineering compound facilitated my arranging for several workers to go to Brigitte's home and crate up her belongings. The staff had suggested the idea. They also arranged to have the large crate shipped to my parents' home in Muskegon, Michigan courtesy of the US Army.

I learned again, when you're nice to people they often look for ways to return the friendliness.

Brigitte informed her boss that she would soon be leaving for America. Together they scheduled her last day.

The boss and her co-workers wanted to meet her American husband so Brigitte promised she would have me stop in to meet them on her last day.

The boss said, "Have him come mid-noon to have coffee with me."

Brigitte told me to bring a small bottle of good Cognac as a gift to her boss.

On the big day I tried to look my best. I found my way, knocked on the door, and was greeted by Frau Barkow.

She ushered me past the curious ladies at work on their machines and into her private parlor. She closed the door, smiled and motioned me to a chair by a coffee table. I handed her the bottle of Cognac which she graciously accepted and set aside. Frau Barkow spoke no English so I knew it would be challenging. It was obvious she expected the ladies to work until she summoned them, so it was me and her. She poured us a coffee and began by asking me about my family and how I would make a living.

The conversation flowed well. She refreshed our coffee and then reached for the bottle of Cognac. She asked if I would like some in my coffee motioning with the bottle. I said yes, took the bottle, removed the seal and removed the cork cap. Frau Barkow was a charming lady. The Cognac warmed the conversation and, when our coffee was done, she replaced the cups with brandy snifters. Through the glass door, I could see Brigitte and her co-workers giving us curious glances.

Aided by the Cognac, Frau Barkow and I had become relaxed and congenial. An hour passed quickly by. The ladies became concerned that we may forget them, so they tapped on the door. Frau Barkow waved them in. I met each of the ladies who gave me curious smiles. It didn't take them long to see that the Cognac had affected the boss more than she realized. They put the bottle discretely away.

Frau Barkow soon realized she was "tipsy." She asked the ladies to take her to her bedroom and help her into bed.

When she was tucked in, she asked them to send me in to say goodbye. I went in. She started to apologize but I put a finger to my lips and shook my head no. I took her two hands in mine, looked her in the eyes, and said, "*Auf Wiedersehen*, Frau Barkow."

She squeezed my hands and smiled. Brigitte and I left to goodbye hugs, tears, and well wishes.

My travel orders had me flying from Berlin to Frankfort. From Frankfort, I would go by military air transport to Andrews Air Force Base in the USA. Then, by air to Ft. Sheridan, Illinois for discharge from active duty.

A week later, Brigitte and Jack would fly from Berlin to Frankfort then on to Detroit where I would meet them. My dad sent me a three-hundred-dollar money order to pay for their travel expenses. My dad was quiet and unpretentious, but he was always there when I needed him.

I made the rounds of Service Company, Special Troops to say goodbye to friends that I had met and soldiered with for my three years in Berlin.

In my forty-two months of total active duty, I soldiered with both volunteers and drafted soldiers. When it came to getting the job done, they all performed equally well. I would trust my well-being to either category without hesitation. It was a true cross section of Americans.

The most notable difference to me was that draftees were often newly, or recently wed. They were suddenly taken away from their new brides or young families to serve two years for Uncle Sam.

They were lonesome and spent much of their leisure time writing their love letters. They were identifiable because the draftees' army serial numbers began with the letters *U.S.*; while volunteers' numbers began with *R.A.*, for Regular Army.

Heading Home

After emotional goodbyes to all my German relatives and friends, I began my flight, over East Germany, at Berlin's Tempelhof Airfield. I landed in Frankfort and reported for my connecting flight to the USA. It was a MATS, military air transportation service flight. The flight was full of families with restless children. The flight was long, and the little ones seemed to wake and cry in shifts.

After a refueling stop in snow bound Gander, Newfoundland and another long flight we landed at Andrews Air Force Base in Maryland.

Although my orders had a connecting flight to Chicago, there was not a specific time or flight specified.

I suspected Andrews AFB was in the general vicinity of Camden, NJ so I found a New Jersey phone book and looked up *Carmen D.*

I found the number and called my former Berlin roommate.

Carmen's mom answered and soon got Carmen to the phone.

"Hello Carmen, this is Lou Schulist, I just arrived here at Andrews from our old stomping grounds, Berlin. I can lay over for a night and visit you if you're open to it."

He said, "I know where you're at. Don't move, I'll be there." Several hours later, Carmen was there. He gave me a vigorous handshake, threw my duffel bag in his trunk and said, "Hop in, we're going to my place." It was his mom's place. Carmen senior, his dad, was deceased. Carmen, still single, was living with his mom. His on again, off again girlfriend must have turned off permanently. I didn't ask about it.

Carmen wasn't surprised to hear I married Brigitte. He was kind of proud that he was instrumental in facilitating the blind date that brought us together.

When we got to Carmen's home, Mama D. was already busy preparing an Italian meal. She warmly welcomed me as "Carmen's army friend."

She showed me to a spare bed and invited me to stay the night. After a generous and delicious meal, Carmen said, "Come on, Lou, I'm going to show you a little of Camden and Philly." He especially wanted me to see *Campbell's Soup*, where his dad was employed his entire working life.

Carmen was obviously proud to tell me that his father had received a certificate of recognition and a cash pay bonus for suggesting an improvement. The suggestion was adopted by the company and improved the flow of the production line Carmen's dad worked on.

After a little sightseeing, we ended up at one of Carmen's neighborhood hangouts.

We re-lived old times in Berlin and chatted with some of the regular patrons. They obviously knew Carmen's fiery Italian temper and as the evening wore on, they enjoyed more and more "pulling his chain."

In Berlin, we frequently had to calm Carmen down as he easily imagined someone was giving him a "dirty look,"

Carmen would grab the table with both hands and say, "Someone hold me back before I go over and kick that guy's butt." He always managed to let us calm him down.

Tonight, became one of those nights. The friendly teasing got to Carmen. He stood up and said, "Lou, let's clean this joint out and teach these guys a lesson. Just like the old days in Berlin."

I replied, "Carmen, we never cleaned out any joints in Berlin and we aren't going to clean out any joints tonight. Drink up, we're leaving."

The locals gave me a friendly, knowing smile as we left.

After a nice breakfast and a goodbye hug from Mama D., Carmen delivered me and my duffel bag to Andrew's Air Force base. Carmen said, "I'll probably never see you again, Lou, thanks for taking time for our visit." We shook hands and said goodbye. Carmen was right, it was our last encounter.

I arranged my air flight direct to Chicago.

At nearby Fort Sheridan, Illinois, I was discharged from active duty and into inactive reserve status. I carefully tucked my DD 214 form with its brief record of my military service and, my Honorable Discharge certificate into my duffle bag. It was March 2, 1959.

Another short DC3 flight across Lake Michigan and I was soon back home on Emerson Avenue in Muskegon.

A heavy March snowfall had made the usual mess of the not-yet-plowed road. Despite this, many family members were there to welcome me home.

It wasn't long before we were seated around the large dining room table eating, drinking, and getting re-acquainted. Of course, the big question was, "When will we meet your bride and your son?"

Several days later, my brother Phil and his wife Barb drove me to Detroit to meet Brigitte's incoming flight. By the time we parked and entered the airport, she had already cleared U.S. Customs. A skycap had seen Brigitte's concerned look and was re-assuring her that he would help her find her way to her waiting party.

Brigitte spotted me and pointed me out to the skycap who smilingly guided her and Jack over to me. I thanked the skycap who waved off the small tip I offered him. He wished us well and left us.

I embraced Brigitte and then introduced her and Jack to the first two of their big, new family.

In Muskegon, a house full of curious family members were anxiously awaiting us as we arrived. Louie's new bride from Germany! Introductions took place with many names to learn and eventually remember.

A second-floor bedroom overlooking the back yard was waiting for us in my parent's home. It was so wonderful to be safely together now in Michigan.

It would be our oasis of privacy for the next several months.

Brigitte was welcomed and treated nicely by all. She easily fit herself into the routine of daily living.

She soon had my mom's kitchen sparkling and efficient and she helped with all my mom's household chores.

Brigitte was picking up English about as quickly as I learned my limited but adequate German.

My dad urged me to relax for several weeks and "rest up from my Army experience."

I said, "No, Dad, it wasn't that bad and now, I have a family to support. I need to get a job immediately and, we want to start looking for a place of our own."

I contacted Continental Motors Corp. regarding the job I had left when I enlisted. They said it was filled, but, because I left in good graces to join the military, they felt obligated to re-hire me. Continental put me back in the aircraft engineering department as an entry level draftsman at the modest salary of one dollar and seventy-five cents per hour.

Although 42 months had passed by, most of the staff I had known were still there. They warmly welcomed me back.

They were all supportive and helpful in getting me started on detailing of simple parts and, on re-draws of tattered and fading part drawings.

I was blessed with a natural intuition for mechanics and eagerly began learning how to detail and dimension simple component parts.

With the help of my military severance pay, I bought a used Chevrolet sedan to get to work, and, to drive Brigitte and Jack around on weekends to become familiar with western Michigan.

Brigitte and I visited the JB Real Estate firm which was near my parent's home. We explained our situation to the owner, Jack, who listened intently and graciously.

We expressed our desire for an appropriate starter home.

Jack said that, although my salary was marginal, he had faith in the security I had working at Continental.

On that basis, Jack agreed he would work with us to find an affordable place to buy. We told him we were not interested in renting and would remain with my parents until we had our own place.

My mom said, "Don't pay rent, rather, make house payments on something simple and affordable. You can always upgrade later." Good advice.

For the next several weeks a friendly, elderly salesman of Jack's firm would pick us up when I returned from work and take us to potential homes for sale.

Because of our low-income status, most of the places we were shown were empty, misused, and often left with trash lying in rooms and on basement floors.

After the fourth or fifth such showing, Brigitte spoke up when the salesman dropped us off at my parents' home.

"Sir," she said. "I will scrub and polish every centimeter of the home we find. But I refuse to accept the dirt, and neglect of people too lazy or too stupid to keep a place clean and in good repair. Please do not show us any more places unless they are reasonably clean and in decent condition."

The surprised salesman replied, "I understand and respect your feelings."

We did not see the salesman for several weeks, although he called several times to reassure us, he was still looking.

Then, an excited call came. "I think I've found the perfect place for you. How soon can I pick you up to look at it?"

It was ideal. It belonged to an elderly widow who took in laundry for a living. She was retiring to a nursing home. The home was an older, small, two-bedroom dwelling with a semi-finished basement that included a nice, but out of character, bar with a large back mirror. The house was clean, in good repair, and in a decent neighborhood of older homes. There was an elementary school within walking distance. It also had an unattached, single stall garage and a small, nicely kept, front and back yard.

The fifty-dollar-a-month payments on a land contract would be manageable but we didn't have the down payment money. We would need three hundred dollars to pay off the widow's equity and take over her land contract.

We didn't have the three hundred and I didn't want to ask my parents. I still wanted to pay back the three hundred dollars dad had sent me for Brigitte's air fare.

How, I wondered, *can we manage this?*

The real estate company's owner, Jack, called and invited us to his office the next day.

He said, "Louis and Brigitte, I have faith in the two of you. If you want this home, I will loan you the down payment. You can pay me back, interest free, as best you can, whenever you can. I will keep track in a notebook in my office desk drawer."

Thus, thanks to another of the "guardian angels" that occurred in our lives, we had our first home.

Soon basic odds and ends of used furniture materialized from relatives. We had our start at independent living and Jack would soon start kindergarten at Marsh School.

We scraped by, living simply. Brigitte had learned to live on simple meals during the war.

We ate a lot of delicious soups, meatloaf with scalloped potatoes, and fresh vegetables. We picked mushrooms and found wild leek. Things I had learned from Mom and Dad.

I brewed my own beer in a stone crock down our basement with a recipe, given me by an uncle, using Blue Ribbon brand malt syrup as a key ingredient.

Brigitte rolled my cigarettes for me and put them in regular packs so my co-workers wouldn't notice.

Sometimes we would splurge and by a sixty-nine-cent bottle of Molly Pitcher wine.

Brigitte told me early on that she needed a sewing machine. She was serious about it because, to her, it was a critical household tool.

We ordered a Ward's Signature sewing machine, on time payments, from the Montgomery Ward catalog.

Brigitte occasionally bought patterns and material, on sale, and made her own lovely dresses She even darned socks that got holes in them. She would hold the sock over her fist as she closed the hole. She had learned, in Germany, how to make things last. Shoes were always kept polished.

I began carpooling with a young co-worker who lived nearby. He and his wife asked if Brigitte would day care their two toddlers, for modest pay, so the wife could take a job. Brigitte agreed to try it out.

My co-worker dropped them off each morning as we met to carpool, and he picked them up again each evening.

When Brigitte began caring for them, they both had quite severe diaper rash. Under her care, the rash began improving quickly and was soon completely gone.

We paid back the three-hundred-dollar loan in just a little over a year, primarily with my first income tax refund. The real estate company owner smiled and shook my hand when he entered zero balance in his spiral notebook.

We thanked him, probably not as profusely as we should have, considering the significant influence he had on our early beginnings.

My salary at Continental barely sustained us. I got paid every two weeks. I often had to borrow a twenty from my dad between paydays. I would repay it on payday only to re-borrow it a week or so later. One time when I was repaying it, Dad said, "Lou, why don't you just keep the twenty. Then you won't have to keep re-borrowing it. It's the same twenty every time."

"Thanks, Dad," I said. "But you know it just doesn't really work that way. I'll just keep borrowing and repaying it until some day when I no longer need to."

Dad smiled and nodded.

I realized that in Berlin, Brigitte had her own money. She helped with family expenses but still had her own spending money. I didn't want her to lose that feeling of financial capability. We agreed that after I paid our fixed expenses, she would get her "house money" to use at her discretion. We agreed that whatever she didn't spend for home needs was hers to keep. As my wages increased, Brigitte's "house money" increased. Brigitte was a cautious shopper who was ever alert for bargains.

She never stinted on things for the home or yard but still managed to save enough to surprise me with thoughtful gifts. Over the years she surprised me with a new 12-foot aluminum fishing boat, a slide projector and viewing screen, an electronic fish finder, a portable ice fishing shanty, most of my "nice" casual clothing, and many other things she knew I would like but probably wouldn't buy for myself.

Herbert and Gertrud

Brigitte stayed in touch with her family, in Berlin, through letters to and from her sister Ellie. They had always been close and had always helped and confided in each other. Ellie apparently also wrote to her brother Herbert in Toronto and had given him our address.

One Sunday morning, our new, not yet listed, phone rang. It was my dad. "Lou, a man called here, asking for Lou Schulist. He speaks broken English but, as I understand, he is here, at the train station on Laketon avenue. He said he is here to pay his sister, Brigitte, a surprise visit. I told him I will send you to pick him up."

I turned to Brigitte, "Your brother Herbert is here, from Toronto, Canada, to visit us."

She immediately reacted. "Gertrud and young Reinhard will be with him. We'll put them in our bedroom. Reinhard can sleep in the small room with Jack, and you and I will make a bed on the living room floor."

It was strange. The first time I saw Herbert was when he answered the door on my first visit to Brigitte's home in Berlin. We weren't even introduced at that time as he called Brigitte to the door, turned away, and disappeared in the room at the end of the hall. That next day, Herbert, his wife Gertrud, and their son Reinhard left for Canada.

Now, here we were, taking them into our home for a week-long visit. We picked them up at the station. They seemed tentative and uneasy until we greeted them warmly with smiles, hugs, and handshakes.

As we rode home, I could sense that Herb was cautiously feeling me out to see how welcome they would be.

Gertrud and Brigitte, of course, knew each other well and were at ease chatting.

Little Reinhard and Jack were quickly getting reacquainted and jabbered in a mix of German and English.

At our home, Herb and Gertrud were pleased to see that we could comfortably accommodate them.

I instinctively liked Herb and felt at ease with him.

As we talked, he loosened up and looked around. He was impressed that we already owned a home. They were still renting in Toronto. Being a skilled trade tool and die maker, Herbert had soon found good employment in Toronto.

He was planning to soon learn to drive, buy a used automobile, and then begin looking for a house in or near Toronto. Herbert told me that he worked with an immigrant Austrian, so they spoke German together and helped each other learn "Canadian." The Austrian, Rudy, and Herbert became close friends and eventually even occasionally hunted and fished together in Canada.

We spent the week introducing them to my family and having picnic outings at several inland lakes.

Herb helped me bottle a batch of my home brew and then enjoyed an occasional bottle as we chatted. It was tricky, we had to sip carefully and leave the last half inch of beer in the bottle to avoid the yeasty sediment on the bottom.

My dad was a founding member and one of the builders of a hunting lodge called Buckhorn Lodge Inc.

It was up north in Newaygo County on seventy-nine wooded acres of prime hunting property which the lodge's founding members had purchased in 1956 for one thousand dollars. Together, mostly on weekends, they built a 28x36 cinder block cabin with a poured concrete floor. It had windows on three walls. On the back wall was a huge fireplace with an opening that could easily accept a three-foot-long log.

The cabin had electric power which allowed an electric stove and several donated, used refrigerators. A rustic setting with comforts. There was an old fuel-oil furnace for back up warmth. Out back and off to one side was an Outhouse. The original well with a handpump was recently upgraded with an electric water pump and underground piping to the cabin. We had a convenient cold-water faucet at our kitchen sink.

We took Herb's family there for an overnight stay.

The lodge had four bunk beds which provided four upper and four lower double beds.

We wandered the woods, drove the back roads, and, in the evening, sat around the wood fire in the big fireplace.

Herb fell in love with Michigan and the Buckhorn lodge.

Living in Toronto with no car, he hadn't yet discovered the natural wonders of Canada. On our walks in the surrounding woods, we kicked up numerous Partridges and saw many deer.

This thrilled the family and fired Herbert up. He had always dreamed of being a *Jägermeister,* a master hunter. Herb suggested that we consider spending an entire week together at the Buckhorn Lodge sometime in the not-too-distant future.

We took Herb's family to the railroad station for their return to Toronto. Herb's first visit was the beginning of our families often joining together. We agreed that, as soon as practical, we would visit them in Toronto.

There was little likelihood of advancement at Continental in the near future so, I went to an employment agency for help in seeking better employment.

The agency advised me that Brunswick, the bowling and billiards company, was adding to their automatic pinsetter engineering staff in Muskegon.

The automatic pinsetter had been designed and, a prototype built, by an engineering company in New York. Many of the design staff hired on with Brunswick and moved to Muskegon where a new plant was built to produce the machines that would replace humans. Another part time job replaced by automation. But for at least the near future years, many more better paying jobs in engineering, manufacturing, shipping, installing and maintenance would result from this invention. Bowling establishments could schedule multiple leagues without worrying about having enough "pin boys."

The Engineering staff of New Yorkers would work along with local new hires, on cost reductions, product improvements, and support of the production operations.

The employment agency arranged an interview for me.

Being employed by the highly respected Continental Motors gave me leverage. The engineering manager who interviewed me said that their New York entourage had toured Continental as part of their introduction to the area.

He told me they were impressed with their high level of engineering and hoped they could hire some of their people away. I secretly felt that I was not yet up to his expectations.

The interview went well until we reached the discussion of money. I was asked my salary expectation. I was making seventy dollars per week or one dollar and seventy-five cents per hour, so I hoped to reach ninety dollars per week at two dollars and twenty-five cents per hour.

"I need to have two dollars and twenty-five cents per hour," I boldly stated.

Wow, I thought, *that will be a fifty cent an hour raise.*

The interviewer said, "We have a problem with that."

My heart sank. He smiled and went on, "The minimum we're offering for a draftsman is two dollars and fifty cents per hour. Can we perhaps convince you to accept the extra quarter because we'd like to have you come work with us, I was hired and would begin, after my two-week notice to Continental. As I left, I looked around at the shiny new offices and the drafting area with its roomy work areas. I'd soon be working in Muskegon's newest engineering and manufacturing facility!"

After giving my two-week notice, I began, in early 1960, what was to be a nineteen-year career with Brunswick Corporation.

The gang at Continental gave me a thick "Machinery's Handbook" as a parting gift. It became a valuable tool.

During my last days at Continental, several individuals came to visit with me at my drafting board. They each quietly and discretely said the same thing. "When you get over to Brunswick, keep an eye open for any more openings. I might be interested in maybe checking it out." They were long-time employees with years of well-paying jobs and health and pension benefits but, human nature is always checking the color of the grass on the other side of the fence.

At Brunswick I reported wearing a white shirt and tie. That was the uniform in the early sixties. Throughout my working career, Brigitte kept my shirts freshly ironed.

I was put right to work. The pinsetter engineering department was in the new facility. The drafting boards were brand new and equipped with the new drafting machines which had horizontal and vertical straight edges which could be rotated for various angles.

I was assigned my work area which had a drawing board, a rotating drafting stool and, behind me, a desk and reference table used mostly for storage. I thought, *Wow, I've got more modern and better equipped working conditions than the Chief Engineer has at Continental.*

The staff, being mostly New Yorkers, spoke loudly and often sarcastically but seemed to be friendly.

They were still busy finding homes and getting involved in Muskegon social circles.

Several of them were into sailing and were excited about the possibilities of our large Muskegon Lake with a channel to Lake Michigan. They were soon involved with the local yacht club activities and social life.

It wasn't long before work conversations became interspersed with discussions on how to design Dock Boxes and planning the weekend sailboat races on Muskegon Lake.

Putting the automatic pinsetter into high production brought out the many hidden design flaws. Many problems were caused by machining tolerances accumulating on parts which had to work together. There were interferences of adjacent moving parts, and cam followers were near falling off their mating cams. It was a busy mechanical device doing many things in proper sequences. Amazingly, it was all powered by one electric motor. In 1960, electronics were still a way off.

As production found problems, the engineering staff redesigned, re-dimensioned, and tweaked tolerances on the offending parts and sub-assemblies. Shims, spacers, and part rework to eliminate local interferences, were used on the production floor to keep dependable, functional, machines going out the door to customers.

It was discovered that I had a gift for tolerance analysis. I was assigned to do analysis on the most complex strings of moving parts. I would mark up part detail prints to recommend re-dimensioning to help the machinist have less dimensional tolerance accumulations.

Also, I would tighten tolerances, as needed, but, within the machinist's equipment accuracy capabilities.

I was soon promoted to the position of Design Checker with a moderate pay raise.

Life was getting more unplanned blessings. I was able to stop home brewing and Brigitte no longer had to roll my cigarettes.

At Continental, the design checkers were all older men. There, I had hoped that I could become a checker before I retired. Here at Brunswick, I became a checker before age twenty-five. Of course, here, I wasn't checking life dependent aircraft engine components and assemblies.

It did show, however, that changing employers can be a significant means of jumping up the ladder.

Brigitte fell in love with America. Although she came from the big city, she quickly acclimated to small town living and, the lakes, streams and forests of West Michigan.

In Berlin, she was limited to freely traveling only within the city's boundaries.

Here with our used auto, we were easily able to travel to nearby towns and even adjoining states.

To give Brigitte a taste of home, I began occasionally driving us to the North side of Chicago for a weekend. We'd leave Jack with my parents. On the North side there were numerous German restaurants, delicatessens, and jewelry shops. Brigitte also enjoyed shopping in the Loop area which we reached by the Elevated train from our Northside hotel.

On a long holiday weekend, we visited my Aunt Helen in Taylorville, Illinois. It was a surprise visit and, I sensed, a bit of a challenge for my Aunt. When she learned we planned to stay two days, she showed us a guest room.

She searched in her refrigerator, found some catfish and re-heated it for us. I told her not to worry about feeding us. We planned to eat simple meals in restaurants. Aunt Helen phoned and let our local cousins know we are visiting. My cousin called, Little Helen, came with her husband, Bill. We sat in lawn chairs in the front yard under a large shade tree. Bill was a tall, dark and handsome and an ex-marine. A dangerous combination. He was assertive and outspoken which visibly bothered my Aunt Helen. She obviously tolerated her son-in-law for her daughter's sake. It didn't take long for Bill to notice Brigitte's attractiveness. He began telling us about the wonderfully productive garden he was raising. He turned to Brigitte and boldly asked, "Would you like to see my garden? I'll take you there now and show you." Brigitte laughed and said, "No thank you Bill, I'd rather stay here with my Lou and visit with your wife." That ended that. Bill didn't seem at all embarrassed, probably figuring it was worth a try. Little Helen must have learned to tolerate his aggressive personality.

We learned two other cousins, Dan and Lawrence, both WWII veterans, were camping on the Sangamon river and catfishing. We went and found them. I introduced Brigitte and Jack and we visited with them there on the riverbank. Danny caught a large frog, tied a string on its back foot and gave it to Jack to play with.

Monday morning, which was the holiday, Aunt Helen insisted on cooking us a nice breakfast of bacon, eggs and toast.

After breakfast, we thanked her for her hospitality and headed back to Muskegon. I made a mental note not to do any more surprise visits.

One evening, I took our son Jack fishing with me. We fished Muskegon lake, from shore, until dark. Jack was excited catching Bluegills. Near dark we began catching Bullheads which are small, dark, catfish with whiskers, wide mouths and beady eyes. Bullheads are armed with three sharp barbs. One on each side of the head and one on top at the back of the head. Many unsuspecting fishermen have received painful and often infected puncture wounds from these barbs.

We kept our fish alive in a large bucket of lake water as we fished.

We came home late, so I took the fish down the basement and put them in cold water in our concrete laundry tub. They were all still alive the next morning so I decided I would refresh the water and clean the fish after work.

About 10:00 am that morning, the phone rang in Brunswick's drafting department.

A co-worker answered, "Lou, it's for you, sounds like your wife."

"Hello," I said. "What's happening?"

"I'll tell you what's happening," Brigitte answered. "What are those ugly things thrashing around in my laundry tub? Please come home at lunch time and get them out of there."

"Those are Bullheads, a special kind of fish," I said.

"I'll clean and skin them after work and we'll fry them up for supper tonight."

"Those ugly things?" Brigitte retorted. "Not in my frying pan."

As I prepared and fried the fish, Brigitte left me alone in the kitchen. As each batch was done, I kept them hot in the oven. When the frying was all done, I invited her to join me. She looked at the platter of golden-brown fish. "I'll try one," she said. The white meat came easily free of the large bones. Without further comment, Brigitte reached for another, and another.

Bullheads became a favorite meal. We often went fishing for them in our earlier years. We would go to a small, nearby lake in the evening, and start a small bonfire for warmth and light. We'd toss out baited set lines and wait.

Sometimes we'd share a bottle of Molly Pitcher wine as we listened to the night sounds and waited in the light and warmth of our small bonfire.

I was solely responsible to clean and fry the fish we caught but Brigitte was willing to help me collect the night-crawlers we used for bait. One evening, after a rainy day, I took her with me to collect bait. She watched me, with my flashlight and bucket, as I grabbed the crawlers which had emerged after dark.

Some would be connected as mating pairs. In the car, on the way home, Brigitte said, "Next time, bring a light and bucket for me too. I'll help you collect them." And she always did.

On one of our many trips to northern Michigan, we stopped at the boat docks in Petoskey to look around.

Brigitte asked me to rig up a fishing pole for her. She wanted to fish off the dock for a little while.

After several minutes, she felt a tug on the pole. She set the hook and had a good time playing the fish. To our surprise she lifted out a nice sized Bullhead.

I took the squirming fish off the hook and raised my arm.

"Stop," Brigitte said sharply. "What do you think you're doing?"

I replied, "I'm going to throw it back."

"You wouldn't throw it back if you caught it," she said. "There's a gallon zip-lock bag in the cooler. Put it in there until we find a place for you to clean it. We're taking it home to eat." Brigitte could be assertive.

I was later glad we did. It provided each of us with a nice sized fillet and was delicious when dusted in flour, salt, pepper and fried golden brown.

Brigitte had three immediate goals. To become an American citizen, to get a driver's license, and, although I had no problem with her Lutheranism, to become a Catholic and practice my religion with me.

She read, studied, and attended applicable classes.

She took citizenship classes at the Hackley building and religion classes at the Catholic Information Center.

I, somewhat impatiently, taught Brigitte how to drive.

Through diligence and determination, she accomplished all three objectives within two years. She did it all in her new language which improved as she went along.

At her citizenship classes, Brigitte met three other young German women. We became friends with them and their spouses and socialized with them over the years. They also led us into meeting other immigrants from Europe.

We had many celebrations with these new Americans.

In November of 1960, our son, Martin, was born.

My job at Brunswick was going well. I continued to be given more responsibilities. I was assigned to be the packaging engineer, first for all pinsetter related products, then, eventually, for all Brunswick division bowling and billiards packaging. I designed, or cost reduced, or improved, packaging for both domestic and overseas shipments. Packaging Engineering is a four-year course at Michigan State University so although I had the title, I certainly was not a fully trained engineer. I admired and envied all the true graduate electrical and mechanical engineers with whom I worked. They were willing to pass on their knowledge and I learned from them on the job.

The specification manuals provided by the various corrugated product manufacturers were full of useful information. They were my packaging textbook. The packaging material suppliers also offered design and testing support, gratis, on request. I used their free and friendly help often. Their engineers were pleased because it helped them justify their customer assistance positions in their companies and got them away from their offices and bosses for a while.

In July 1963, my dear older brother, Leonard, passed away from a blood clot due to a broken leg and the poor circulation resulting from his diabetes. Leonard laid in the hospital several weeks after falling and breaking his leg with a compound fracture. On a Sunday, I left Brigitte home with our newborn baby daughter, Dierdre. Jack stayed home also to help.

I went to church service with young Martin. On the way home, I suddenly decided to visit Leonard. I was near the hospital and I hadn't seen him since he fell and was injured. I told little Martin to sit quietly in the car and look out the window. I would be right back. I cracked a window, locked the car and hurried into the hospital.

As I entered Leonard's room, he was resting quietly. There was a soft, warm breeze blowing through a nearby window.

I sat by his bedside and softly said his name. Leonard opened his eyes, smiled and reached out his hand to me.

I told him about his new niece, Dierdre, born that June. After we chatted quietly, I told him I had to leave now because I left little Martin alone in the car. Leonard said, "I'm glad you're my brother, Lou." Then he looked at me and said, "Goodbye, Lou."

We didn't casually use the word "love" in those days but we both felt it.

Dad called me early the next morning to tell me Leonard passed away during the night. I was thankful that I had been given the opportunity to say, what I didn't know would be, my last goodbye.

My dad was also quite happy to hear that I had visited Leonard in his last hours.

Diabetes was poorly controlled in those days. They've come a long way in treating the disease since then.

Back then, my mom sharpened Len's injection needles with emery cloth and kept them in alcohol for re-use.

Len would have his Glucose level checked once a month by his doctor. His daily insulin dose level for the entire month would be based on that one reading. He often went into shock and would be hospitalized several days.

I was haunted in my young years by fear of Leonard's dying. I had prayed for him more often than I prayed for any other reason.

Brunswick provided another employee opportunity. Employees were offered a discounted company stock purchase plan through payroll deduction. I participated and, because the pinsetter market was still relatively young and growing, the stock appreciated nicely.

In January of 1965, I was promoted with an unusual title of Chief Design Checker and Packaging Engineer. With it, came additional responsibility to assign and supervise the work of the designers, drafters, and checkers.

Also, another token raise in pay. I now made enough to live comfortably and to enjoy a simple life.

I was more interested in my family living a fulfilling and happy life than in accumulating wealth so, in 1965, I asked Brigitte if she would like us to visit her family in Berlin. She had been away from them for six years now. She said, "Yes, if we can afford it."

We cashed in the accumulated shares and had enough to fly with KLM airlines and have enough expense money.

That summer, Brigitte and the three children stayed with her mom, in Berlin, for four weeks. I had two weeks of paid vacation, so I went a week later and returned a week sooner. The Berlin family members confessed they were surprised that our marriage had lasted and prospered.

Because of Brigitte's independent and assertive nature, they predicted among themselves that our marriage wouldn't survive much more than a year or two.

None of Brigitte's Berlin family were practicing Christians. They couldn't anticipate that because of my foundation in faith and, Brigitte's becoming active in practicing and strengthening her faith, we had the help and blessings of the Almighty.

Though at times we tested the ties that bind, we two had become "one" as He intended.

While waiting for me to join her in Berlin, Brigitte took our three children and walked the several blocks to the home of her old friend Irma.

She knocked on the door and waited, wondering if Irma still lived there at home with her mother. Irma answered the door. Brigitte said she looked confused for a moment then, exclaimed, "Brigitte, it's you!" She invited them in.

She remembered Jack and was surprised to meet Martin and little Dierdre. Irma told Brigitte that she too was near to marriage several times but each time her mother went into a setback on her heart problems and begged Irma to stay with her and care for her.

After I arrived, we enjoyed several family gatherings with relatives, including some from Leipzig which was in East Germany. Because of their age and the fact that they owned a small farm they were not considered a flight risk. The Berlin wall was now erected but the other family members lived in West Berlin.

I flew back home alone one week earlier and was waiting in Detroit when Brigitte and the children arrived.

Back home in Muskegon, we returned to our routines.

Jack began grade school at St. Michaels. I'd drop him off on the way to Brunswick and he'd walk the approximately three miles home. He had a schoolmate who accompanied him most of the way. Brigitte took care of our home and the two young ones.

Brigitte told me that, with our growing family, we should consider looking for a new, larger home. She emphasized the word "new." Brigitte was now a confident and assertive partner blessed with common sense and a woman's motherly instinct for hearth and home.

She was tireless in caring for and improving all we had. I was happy that she was happy to be a stay-at-home mom. I wanted my children to grow up in the same kind of home environment that I did. That was far more important to me than getting rich beyond our modest needs. We needed her home more than we needed her any income.

I remembered, as a child, how sad I had been when, for a short time during the war, my mom began to work the second shift at the Amazon Knitting Mills.

I would sit by the back window watching the city buses come and go until she would step off one and walk up our back path. As soon as she was through the door, I was happy again. Mom saw how we all missed her and soon quit.

I think we underestimate the benefit and power of mom's presence in the home, especially for the kids.

No amount of wealth or possessions can compensate for the loss of that anchor. Stay at home moms and larger families were common in those days of simpler lives.

I don't remember any mom working outside the home in my old Muskegon neighborhood.

Brigitte's boundless energy, to mow the lawn, plant and maintain flowers and shrubs, shovel snow, wash and polish the car, cooking, cleaning, sewing, ironing my white shirts and, keeping a comfortable clean home, was a wonder to family and friends.

In retrospect, I took it too much for granted and I'm sure she would have liked to hear more words of sincere appreciation and acknowledgment.

I recall one instance where my strong feelings toward having a stay-at-home wife was tested. In 1964 we had purchased a new Pontiac Catalina nine passenger station wagon in a shade of gold. The payments made money a little tight. I saw that a Bowling alley nearby was advertising for a night waitress working a six to twelve shift. We reasoned if Brigitte worked, I could watch the kids. Brigitte said, "If you want me too, I will do it." We called and were asked to come in for an interview. The manager looked at Brigitte and listened to her German accent. "Yes, I think you would be fine for the job. Let's go out on the lanes and I'll show you the area you will take care of." He walked us around explaining the job.

As we were returning to his office a bowler shouted to the manager, "Wow, is that our new waitress?"

The manager laughed and replied, "I hope so."

The bowler then yelled, "Did you tell her that Thursday nights are topless?"

That was the end of that. I said, "Come on Hon, this isn't for you. We don't need this income."

On the way home, Brigitte said, "Thank you, I agree, I'd rather stay home and wait on you and the kids. I know we'll do ok and let's start enjoying that beautiful new station wagon."

We began looking at various builder's speculation homes in the Muskegon County area. We found a new, three-bedroom, ranch style home on a large corner lot in Whitehall, north of Muskegon. It was within reasonable commuting distance for me.

The builder was opening this new development and was anxious to sell this home and continue expanding.

He visited our home and proposed a smooth path to get us into a new eighteen-thousand-five-hundred-dollar ranch house with affordable monthly payments.

The builder bought our first home which had appreciated in value. He paid off the land contract and applied our equity as down payment on our first brand new home.

We were able to take immediate possession and move in.

In 1966, I began commuting from Whitehall to Muskegon.

Jack and Martin began attending Whitehall school and in February of 1967 our son Michael was born.

It was at that time Brigitte announced to me, "I'm going to have a husband who doesn't smoke, I hope it can be you. I don't want this baby and our other kids living in a smoker's smelly home."

After twenty-eight years of smoking, I quit. Not easy.

My brother-in-law, Chuck, who was in real estate, was always finding deals. He found our first used TVs for us.

Now, he showed us a used Ford Fairlane which was clean, in good shape and affordable. Brigitte wanted it and got it. Brigitte now had her own wheels. Now she was free to shop, go to the kids' daytime school functions and enjoy the feeling that comes with being mobile.

In 1972, our youngest, Michael, began kindergarten. He hopped on the school bus for the first time, wearing German lederhosen.

With me commuting, it fell to Brigitte to take the kids to and from after school activities.

When they became involved in sports, she attended the various competitions.

The kids began coming home from school and reporting that other kids were telling them "how pretty their mom is."

Brigitte was not the hug and kiss type of Mom. She showed her love by timely daily meals, clean, pressed cloths, fresh, comfortable beds, an orderly home and a caring discipline. The kids all helped with kitchen chores.

Together we traveled, camped, fished, hunted and grew up. The children enjoyed their many cousins and our great family gatherings over the years. They also made childhood friends at co-worker family gatherings.

The new, Brunswick operation brought together many young people of various skills. We had engineers, draftsmen, material planners and skilled craftsmen in the model shop and test labs. We interacted in our work and became socially connected. We soon were playing friendly jokes and ribbing each other.

A young engineer, Tom, became our social sparkplug.

I took him Bullhead fishing and invited him and his wife to a Bullhead fish dinner. It was a big hit and gave Tom the idea for a Bullhead excursion with our colleagues. It was a big deal. We had two sixteen-foot motorboats that were trailered to our site.

I and one other, older, participant, Joe, knew the routine. The two of us supervised the making of two long set lines with twelve, evenly spaced number four hooks and then, baiting them with small liver chunks.

The lines each had a heavy weight at each end. Attached to one end was a line long enough to reach the surface and attached to it was a one-gallon plastic milk carton as a bobber to locate the line.

Each boat took a setline out and placed it slightly offshore in about four to six feet of water.

We drank beer around a rousing wood bonfire as we waited for dusk. Bullheads bit best from dusk to around Midnight.

About an hour after dusk, we ran the lines for the first time. As we pulled in the marker lines, we could feel the fish tugging below on the set lines.

Most hooks had fish. We took them off, rebaited if needed, and reset the lines. We knew we were flirting with the fishing laws, but Bullheads were considered a trash fish by those put off by the appearance and reputation for being a lowly bottom-feeder. What they didn't know was that in the Spring and early Summer, with all their body fat used up, the flesh was delicious and came easily off the large rib bones.

The gang watched fascinated as Joe and I deftly gripped each fish by the head carefully avoiding the barbs. We made a circular cut through the skin just behind the head.

We then slit the skin along the back barb to provide a skin flap. Using water-pump pliers we gripped the skin flap and pulled the skin down from head to tail in one smooth motion. We then gutted them, cut off the heads and removed the barbs. After running a thumb along the inside backbone to remove any offal, and then rinsing them clean, they were ready for frying.

By now our fire had nice coals which we raked into a flat stack. We put the fish in a large plastic bag with a dry fish coating and coated them.

Tom had relatives in the sheriff's department which allowed him to borrow a large, deep three-foot diameter frying pan from the jail's kitchen.

A half-gallon of canola oil, smoking hot, quickly turned the fish to an irresistible golden brown.

Tentative and uncertain samplings quickly became hearty appetites along with random snacks and beers.

The early summer "Bullheader" became an annual event.

We also had many family events where the wives and kids were included. These often took place around a bonfire in Tom's yard.

Tom owned a large old house on acreage so, there was lots of room and no near neighbors to bother.

Tom and his wife were Irish Catholics. They were very efficient in populating the world with delightful Irish children in close succession.

The children all ran wildly and joyfully around the property while the parents visited.

Often there would be large, gutted, but whole twenty plus inch Lake Michigan lake trout stuffed with a delicious oyster stuffing and wrapped in heavy foil roasting in the coals. We also added foil wrapped potatoes to bake in the coals.

As we waited, we joked, flirted and admired each other's wives.

Tom always intuitively knew when the fish was done and ready to enjoy. The oyster stuffing was a delicacy and the meat pulled cleanly off the bones in big, tasty chunks.

These get togethers, of course, were weekend treats.
For our kids, Monday's meant, back to school. They did well in track and enjoyed school activities.
The teen years tested us all, but we all survived.

When the kids had reached the age that they were all in school, Brigitte would often meet me for lunch, in Muskegon, at one of the several wonderful Greek restaurants. Her Ford was always kept spotless and shiny.

Whitehall and it's connecting neighbor city, Montague, were popular tourist destinations due mostly to beautiful White Lake which connected to Lake Michigan. I joined the White Lake VFW, which was very active, led mostly by WWII veterans at the time. I was eligible because I had earned the Berlin Occupation Medal. They had regular weekend dinner dances with live area bands. The large dance floor was always comfortably crowded with dancing couples. We made numerous interesting and colorful acquaintances there over the years. I heard frequent comments on Brigitte's charming accent and pleasant personality. Brigitte loved to dance, and I was getting better at it, I think.

We danced every Polka, but I always preferred the slow dances. The slow dances always reminded me of finding and courting Brigitte in Berlin.

We attended St. James Catholic church in Montague. Brigitte and I soon joined the small choir. It was the first of three successive church choirs we would experience.

Brigitte commented several times over the years on how being in the choir made the Easter and Christmas seasons so much more meaningful.

The preparation and the various seasonal church services highlighted the true meaning of the religious seasons.

Also, choirs have a way of becoming close families in themselves.

It was a short drive to White Lake, so we often took the family there and fished for bluegills. We fished from the shore during the spring and summer and out on the ice during the winter. I cleaned and cooked a lot of fish.

We often cooked outdoors with a bonfire in our big backyard. On summer nights we'd marvel at the Milky Way and often, Aurora Borealis, the beautiful northern lights. Because we were one of the earlier families in the area, we had little light pollution at night.

In 1975, my mom urged me to check into the G.I. Bill.

Mom told me that my brother-in-law, Mel, was getting paid for attending college level classes through the G.I. Bill.

Mel served a four-year enlistment in the Air Force during the Vietnam war and was deployed there for a short time.

I investigated and I learned that, through my service, I was G.I. bill eligible for college classes.

I enrolled at Muskegon Business College and began with business law, accounting, and statistics classes.

All were evening, after work, classes.

I discovered that I now loved learning. My exposure to the world of manufacturing and engineering made me aware of the value of this knowledge.

As I learned, it gave me confidence to relate to Brunswick's management personnel more comfortably.

I was pleasantly shocked when I went into the College office to receive my first month's G.I. Bill payment. It was a check for four hundred tax free dollars. It increased my monthly income by fifty percent and was an unexpected blessing.

Because Brunswick's policy was to pay college tuition for employees taking relevant classes, it was pure profit and my first significant discretionary income.

I bought cheap, used textbooks. My real cost was the devotion of my time to classes and many hours of study.

Brigitte saw my commitment and was supportive.

Slowly, we began to buy, on time, furniture upgrades and a new washer and dryer, so, she realized the college financial support had benefits.

I studied mostly at lunch time at work, and, at home lying on the living room floor with the family carrying on around me. When we traveled, my books went with me. I was working toward a BS in the field of business management.

I aced all my subjects except for college algebra. Although it was one of my favorite studies, I only managed a C+.

After several years, my G.I. bill eligibility and pay ended, but, because Brunswick paid the tuition and I wanted to learn, I continued my college courses.

Besides the helpful income, the G.I. bill had a major, positive impact on my life. Another unexpected blessing.

Knowledge is power in many ways. Not only in the application but also in the acquired confidence.

I greatly enjoyed my college classmates who were mostly in their late teens and early twenties.

Being in my late thirties, and usually wearing a tie and jacket, they treated me with both respect and curiosity.

Our kids bought a letter home announcing that Whitehall High School was beginning an evening class program for adults who hadn't yet received their high school diploma.

Brigitte was interested. She was interviewed and tested, and it was determined that her German schooling equated to a Michigan tenth grade level. Brigitte enrolled in the program and began attending night classes in History, English, Math, and even a shop class.

She studied diligently and was occasionally frustrated due to the minor language barrier. Brigitte polished her English in earlier days by listening to the *Today* show as she did her household chores.

In May of 1976, wearing a long dress she had made special for the occasion, Brigitte, along with approximately thirty other adult students, proudly received her Whitehall High School diploma at a special evening ceremony. Brigitte valued her high school diploma second only to her United States citizenship certificate.

At Brunswick, around 1978, I was approached by a Minnesota packaging machine building company with their idea to partially automate the packaging of individual bowling balls.

I took them to the ball plant to observe the manual operation. They took notes and pictures and several weeks later returned with drawings and a proposal for a machine that would form the die cut box blanks and hot melt glue the bottom closed.

They also redesigned the corrugated ball box to a cost reduced version which still had the required take home carrying handle for use by the customer.

I proposed the project to Brunswick's manufacturing engineers for a feasibility study.

The engineers determined that the labor, material savings and space requirements provided a favorable payback period so, the project was approved.

Several months later, I received notice the machine was built. I was asked to come to Alexandria, Minnesota to observe a trial run and approve the machine for delivery.

I spent several days at the factory observing the test runs and assuring myself of the ease of operation and consistent performance without downtime. Their engineer and sales representative were both happy because they could take me to breakfast, lunch, and dinner at a nice local restaurant at their company's expense.

The machine performed as expected so it was accepted for delivery to Brunswick.

My return flight from Minneapolis had a layover at O'Hare in Chicago. As I was strolling down an airport corridor, I heard a voice call out, "Hey Lou, Lou Schulist." Sitting in a waiting area was a former Brunswick manager, Dave M. "You headed for Muskegon?" he asked.

I was, and so was he. We determined we were on the same flight.

Dave said, "We've got about an hour wait, let's go get a beer and bratwurst."

As we sat enjoying our treat he asked, "How are things at Brunswick." We had recently been assigned a new plant manager who was unfriendly and abrasive. He was the reason Dave and numerous other managers and engineers had left Brunswick for friendlier employers.

Dave told me he was now the vice-president of engineering at an up-coming office furniture manufacturer named Haworth. It was in Holland Michigan about thirty-five miles South of Muskegon.

Dave told me Haworth was growing fast. They were expanding their engineering department and hiring a fair number of draftsmen and designers.

He said they needed a chief draftsman to supervise the draftsmen and technical illustrators. Dave said he had thought about possibly contacting me. He asked me to come in for a discussion of the position. We agreed to meet at Dave's office the following Saturday.

Dave knew I had the relevant experience and job knowledge, so it was a question of salary. Would it justify driving approximately fifty miles each way?

The offer was nearly double my Brunswick salary.

I discussed the opportunity with Brigitte.

Commuting the thirty to forty minutes to Brunswick was already a wasted time inconvenience. Now the time would be doubled at both ends, morning and evening.

I reasoned to Brigitte, "Brunswick Pinsetter is now a matured operation, and I'm probably at the top of my career there. Raises are small and infrequent.

"I know, and I trust Dave. I would feel secure working in his department. Also, Dave mentioned we could car-pool. We would connect in Muskegon where he lived."

Brigitte said, "It sounds like a good opportunity. Let's try it. When our Michael graduates, he will want to be on his own. You know, he has his independent streak and self-confidence."

Yes, I agreed, that was already plainly obvious.

Brigitte continued, "When we have our empty nest, we can look for a new home in Holland."

In 1979, after nineteen years of employment, I resigned from Brunswick and began my career at Haworth.

I had matured and learned a lot at Brunswick. I had no plans or desire to leave, they had treated me very well. It seemed however, that this opportunity was meant to happen.

Meeting Dave, by chance, was another of those unplanned happenings which so significantly affected my life. Again, "Someone" must have planned it for me.

Haworth was the first job where I sat at a desk rather than a drawing board.

It was a growing company and, because they often promoted from within, opportunities abounded.

I was effective at leading my work groups and so I was assigned more responsibility as time went on.

One of the most significant opportunities was an assignment to form a team and devise a plan to provide special, non-catalog products requested by customers.

Our focused team of several product and manufacturing engineers, and material planners developed a plan for a low volume operation to receive customer requests for specials, design them, and produce them.

We proposed an engineering and material planning staff and an offline metal and wood machining and assembly capability.

The company approved and financed the enterprise.

The office and factory space, staffing and equipment were allocated and quickly became operational.

It proved highly effective. Not only did the willingness to provide specials leverage our winning of contracts for standard products against our large, established competitors, but the specials in themselves were priced to be profitable.

I often received complements on our success and accomplishments but in honesty, I confessed that I deserved little of the credit. The several managers and shop supervisors who reported to me were knowledgeable, and respected by their staffs.

The bright and eager, mostly young, staff of engineers, designers, drafters, material planners and skilled laborers rightly deserved the credit. They eagerly attacked every opportunity and always came up with a solution or viable alternative to every challenge.

I knew that in their individual specialties they knew far more than me. I managed by observing the results.

I stayed out of their way except to help them if possible, with any arising needs. They appreciated their freedom to perform and did so enthusiastically.

I remembered as a young draftsman how I longed for recognition and complements. I watched for every opportunity to genuinely use this powerful motivating tool.

Throughout the 1980s and 90s, Haworth grew within the contract office furnishing trade.

They introduced many new and innovative products.

They expanded, acquired related businesses, and became a global competitor. Specials continued to be a key strategy and the volume of specials grew accordingly.

On my annual vacations, Brigitte and I traveled. We preferred our pickup truck and used secondary roads when practical. We liked small town meat markets and bakeries.

We'd buy homemade cold cuts and hard rolls and park in a corn field or meadow for a picnic. We seldom made reservations which gave us flexibility to stop and linger when and where we wanted.

If we couldn't find lodging, we'd sleep in the pickup's eight-foot bed with its fiberglass topper. Brigitte sewed a mattress cover for a six-inch thick, four foot by six-foot foam rubber pad. It looked like a factory-made mattress. We had a cozy double sleeping bag, pillows and camping supplies ready if needed.

Sleeping in the pickup in a remote campground or a state or county park was a treat.

Several memorable adventures, among the many, were a three-week motor trip through the Canadian maritime provinces, a trip around Lake Superior, and a visit to the Cape Cod area. All had unexpected surprises mostly resulting in good experiences. We always began our trips with a prayer asking for safety, adventure, and the joy of God's creation. We were always blessed with more than we expected. In earlier days we often flew to vacation spots but, over time, we discovered that unscheduled travel by automobile provided the freedom and opportunity to relax, enjoy and experience what's "out there."

In her citizenship and high school classes Brigitte had studied American history. As we traveled, she noticed signs indicating significant Historic sites and would urge me to turn off the highway and visit them. We spent an entire day at Gettysburg. We also visited numerous other Civil War sites. Herself, having experienced the horrors of war, Brigitte could sense the drama of these battles.

As a young German girl, Brigitte enjoyed reading novels about the American West and our cowboy heroes.

I knew a trip out West would be a treat to her. A chance to see and experience the part of America she read about as a young girl in Germany.

We flew to Phoenix; Arizona then rented a car. We traveled secondary roads as much as possible to the Grand Canyon, Flagstaff, then the Oak Creek Canyon road to Sedona. From Sedona we visited Prescott, then Tucson, Nogales, Mexico and eastward to Tombstone. Along the way we stayed in the small retirement community of Green Valley a little south of Tucson. We were impressed by its laid-back ambiance and well-organized activity possibilities for retirees.

Numerous developers were active in the area.

We looked around at locations and at model homes.

We had visited Florida several times and considered the possibility of a winter retirement place there.

We liked the dryer Arizona weather better and the ability to easily travel any direction to adjoining states or into Mexico. The Florida peninsula was somewhat limited in that respect.

We selected a site and a model in a development called The Springs at Santa Rita. Building of our winter retirement home would begin in the Spring of 1997.

Haworth had one more challenging assignment for me.

They were having trouble in recruiting the growing number of factory members they needed to keep up with the growth of the company.

Because of the limited supply of unemployed labor prospects in the Holland area, and I'm sure other important considerations, they decided to build a large metal fabrication factory in a small university town of Big Rapids, eighty-five miles north of Holland.

A woman was hired as the Plant Manager to oversee construction and then, to start up operations and run the plant. Her aggressive and commanding style was effective in dealing with construction company personnel and manufacturing equipment suppliers.

She also had the support of various skilled individuals from the Holland headquarters. She appreciated their support but let them know she was in charge. Any final decisions would be hers.

When the plant became operational and had been running for several months it was not accomplishing the important goal of filling orders for the metal products.

The plant manager's "hands on" control and involvement, which had served so well in the early phases of construction and start up, was now hampering the actual manufacturing and assembly operations.

Line Supervisors who should be co-operating and working with each other to maximize throughput were forced to work through the plant manager who wanted to be involved in every decision and to personally solve every problem.

Supervisors began to experience quality problems, delays, and shortages which they weren't free to solve.

Company executives felt a change of leadership style was needed in the plant operations.

I was told by the director of manufacturing that the present plant manager was going to be terminated and I was selected to replace her. I was to begin immediately. I could only guess that because I received credit for the startup and success of the specials operation it was hoped that I could help get the remote metals plant profitable and shipping on time.

I went home and told Brigitte, "They want me to take over management of the new one million square foot metals plant up north."

She responded with her standard first response, "Oh my…"

I continued, "They will arrange a continuously reserved room for me at the local Holiday Inn and you can join me there. All our expenses will be paid by the company."

Brigitte replied, "I'll visit you there occasionally and we can go out for dinner, but I won't leave my home unattended for weeks to sit in a hotel room."

"And" she continued, "You tell them you will spend your weekends home."

That's how we did it and it worked out well.

As I traveled north on my first day, I wondered what lie ahead. Here I am, some college education but no degree, assigned to walk in and take over a staff and a plant operation vital to the company.

Well, I thought, *this must be meant to be. He put me in this predicament and it's up to Him to see me through it.*

Somehow up to now He always has. I had no plan but to see what's there and deal with it. I knew I had an upcoming first chance to make an important first impression.

I arrived at 7:30 am. The human resources manager greeted me and showed me to the plant manager's office.

She told me the office staff and factory supervisors would be in the large adjacent conference room at 8:00 am to meet with me. At the appointed time, I entered and stood at the front of the room. I looked around, smiled, and began by introducing myself.

I complemented the previous manager for bringing the plant online and hiring capable people. I told them that over the coming weeks I looked forward to becoming better acquainted with them, and their roles, individually.

I explained that we share the challenge of making this state-of-the-art plant run smoothly and profitably.

I told them that making this plant successful would mean good paying jobs for this community for the foreseeable future. Hopefully, it could provide opportunities for their children and even their grandchildren over time.

Over the next several days I made essentially the same speech to all shifts at factory meetings.

One important rule I remembered. Don't ever try to lie to hourly workers or skilled trades. You won't get away with it. First and foremost, people must trust you if you want them to do their best.

In closing with my new staff, I used the logic which served well in Specials. I complemented them that each of them knew their specific job far better than I. They didn't need my permission to "get out there and get it done." I'll stay out of their way, but I will be watching for results.

I encouraged them to ask their factory workers for their ideas for improving quality and productivity and to not be afraid to make the decision to implement improvements.

If they need my help, come see me, no appointment needed.

For the near future, we would hold a short, daily, 7:00 am all hands staff meeting to allow for problem solving interaction between the inter-dependent departments.

A significant problem was downtime of the complicated, state of the art, fabricating equipment and powder coat painting equipment.

The previous plant manager believed all maintenance personnel should be familiar with all equipment, so she ordered that they be on a periodic rotation schedule between the various fabricating and assembly areas including a separate, nearby wood product operation.

It was a noble concept, but it was too soon for it in a new factory with new equipment and maintenance people just learning the new operations and equipment.

As a result, no one mastered the intricacies of the individual machines, no one took ownership or responsibility for performance, and no one could be held accountable.

The rotation practice was stopped. Accountability and expectations were assigned for each area.

After a brief and concentrated learning period, performance and dependability improved markedly and soon was acceptable and effective.

A knowledgeable material manager from the main plant was temporarily assigned to the metal components plant.

He successfully hammered home the concepts of *just-in-time* and *zero defects.* He taught the operators that "their customer," was the next workstation. He said, "Take pride in sending your customer the needed components on time with no defects."

His contribution was basic to the ensuing success.

After approximately three months, the plant accountant smilingly told me the plant had become profitable.

This material manager was a key factor in the success.

I informed executive management that I intended to retire December 31st, 1998.

They asked me to review the various staff members and recommend a candidate to replace me as plant manager.

There was one local area material manager who, without being asked, immersed himself in the entire plant operations. He was skilled at seeking out workstations that hindered a smooth, continuous, product flow. Where he saw a problem, he diplomatically involved himself and helped solve it. He informally kept me appraised of his activities. I could see he was effective and making an important contribution. I stayed out of his way. He became recognized and accepted as a trusted advocate in all areas of the factory.

He was low key in his approach and always gave the credit for improvements to the involved factory workers.

Most importantly. He had the respect and trust of the office staff and, the floor supervisors and workers.

I recommended him as my replacement and, after being interviewed by company executives, he was chosen.

He ran the steel components plant successfully and later was promoted to additional corporate responsibilities.

Shortly before retirement, I was offered one more, very tempting, opportunity. The V.P. of manufacturing asked me to go to Sydney, Australia for one year and manage a plant they had recently acquired. I was to instill Haworth company principles and groom a replacement from the staff. It was a Friday and he asked me to think about it over the weekend.

I told Brigitte we had an opportunity to live a year in one of the great cities of the world, Sydney.

I explained the details of the offer to her. We were both excited at the prospect.

Saturday morning, I was sitting in our family room looking out at the Fall colors beginning to emerge.

Brigitte joined me with a coffee for each of us.

As we sipped, she began, "You know, for the last several months you've talked about how tired you are of holding staff meetings, department meetings, plant meetings, and making status presentations to the executives. And we've talked about how we look forward to our first winter of retirement in our new home in Arizona."

She took a deep breath and continued, "We don't need to see another big city. After a couple of months, the charm will wear off and we will wish we were back in our own private world. I think you should refuse their request. Let's begin our retired life together and try to enjoy our remaining years as we planned."

"You're right," I said, "You've summed it all up nicely and I agree."

Brigitte smiled and said, "I'll get us another coffee."

Monday morning, I was waiting outside the office of the vice president. I followed him into his office and, without bothering to sit down, thanked him for the opportunity and the implied trust in my abilities.

"But" I told him, "I will pass up this opportunity and retire December 31st as I planned."

He nodded, and said, "I understand your decision."

The director, that I reported to directly, told me, "Lou, after about six months, you are going to be bored with retired life. Come and see me and we'll put you to work as a consultant. There's always someplace that can use some experienced help and you can make some good money."

He was wrong. My life with Brigitte had been anything but boring and I anticipated the best was yet to come. We neither needed nor wanted more money, especially at the expense of our uninterrupted time together.

I never went back, nor sought more income by any means. We were too busy living and the best things in life were almost free.

Raising our four children in the 70s and 80s was a joy and at times a challenge. Thankfully, we didn't need to deal with the intricacies of social media. But, with anti-war and anti-racism protests going on in our country there were many social forces at work to influence the thinking of impressionable young people.

Brigitte was the disciplinarian. She saw things as more directly being right or wrong.

Having been raised by lenient parents, in a large family, I was more inclined to have a tolerance for ambiguity.

The kids commented they'd rather be spanked by dad than by mom although the boys said their early years of wearing Lederhosen provided good spanking insulation.

Our differing approaches caused some disagreements between Brigitte and me during our kid's adolescent and teen years. We worked hard at compromise.

We sometimes tried "tough love" but, thankfully, plain love eventually prevailed and continues to work to this day.

We all survived and grew and learned together. The children became educated, found good employment, and, with a few bumps along the way, found their soul mates.

As my four adult children entered the world of work and business, I gave them the benefit of a lesson I had learned over the years. I advised them, "Before you go into any meeting, ask yourself, what is my objective here? Fix that objective firmly in your mind and don't get sidetracked by emotion or pride or get drawn into a non-productive 'pissing contest.' They all claim to have benefitted by that discipline. Also, I cautioned them, if you attain any supervisory role, resist the temptation to be a 'boss.' You are a cheerleader and an enabler. If your team members succeed, you succeed."

With all four children raised and doing well, we were ready to fully experience retired life.

We looked forward to good times with our family and friends during spring, summer and early fall in beautiful Michigan.

And we anticipated making new acquaintances and seeing the sights of the Southwest. We looked forward to having our children and their families visiting us in Green Valley, Arizona during our winters there.

Grand children began enriching our lives. I enjoyed taking my young grandsons fishing. I'd put a couple of them on the front seat of my pickup truck with me and we'd go find a suitable spot for hook and bobber fishing for panfish. I'd regale them with untrue stories of my mighty feats. They'd listen intently not sure what all to believe.

Chris liked to fish from the dock at a nearby Yacht Club which he pronounced yachett club. That's what the sign said.

As we were getting our tackle out of the truck, Chris spotted my old misshapen, leather hat with the curled brim. He said, "Grandpa, don't forget your hat."

I said, "Thanks Chris but I'm getting afraid to wear that hat."

"Why grandpa?" he asked.

"Because," I said, "when I wear that, too many people mistake me for Indiana Jones and bother me for an autograph."

I put the hat on and said, "There, don't I look like Indiana Jones?" He studied me seriously for a moment.

"I don't know Grandpa" he answered, "Maybe just the hat."

Then as I took out my well used rod and reel, I said, "Here's another thing, I have to keep a close watch on this fishing rod."

"Why," Chris asked.

"Because," I said, "They're trying to get it away from me to put it into the Fisherman's Hall of Fame Museum."

We caught a dozen "keeper" bluegills that day.

Back home in the backyard, I set up a board on two sawhorses on which to clean the fish.

I told Chris, "Stand here and watch and you'll learn how to scale and fillet a fish." He watched me work through several fish and soon lost interest. He wandered away, found a broken hickory shovel handle in the shed and began smacking trees with it. He then began hitting our large 8-foot by 8-foot stack of oak firewood logs. He glanced at me to check my reaction.

I said, "You better be careful, you might wake that thing up."

"What thing?" he asked.

"I don't know," I answered. "I was walking by the woodpile a few days ago and heard some kind of growling or moaning sounds coming from the pile. I carefully looked in between the logs and saw something move. Whatever it was, looked toward me. It had beady red eyes and snarled showing two long yellow fangs. Then, it turned and disappeared somewhere in that big stack of logs."

Chris stood holding the stick and staring at the woodpile. I said, "Why don't you put down the stick and try reaching in there with your arm. I think he had fur and maybe you can pet him."

"NO WAY HOSAY!" Chris shouted back.

I said, "It's starting to get a little dark. Go ask Grandma for a flashlight. Maybe, with a flashlight, you can spot him and see him for yourself."

Chris ran to the patio door, knocked on it, and called for Grandma. Brigitte came and opened the door to him.

Chris said, "Grandma, Grandpa said you should quick give me a flashlight so I can look into the woodpile. Maybe I will see that wild thing with the yellow fangs that's hiding in there." Brigitte looked over at me and shook her head.

The flashlight and woodpile kept Chris busy until I was finished cleaning the fish and putting things away.

Our grand kids were all special, each in their own way.

One windy day I told my then little granddaughter Rachele, "It's so windy outdoors that the wind blew my ears off, but I quick turned my head around and it blew them right back on again." Rachele looked at my ears then said, "Grandpa, that can't be true. If that had happened your ears would now be on backwards."

On another occasion, my five-year-old grandson, Kodi, was sitting next to me in my easy chair. I saw he was studying a canvas, signed, limited issue, reproduction of the Greg Olsen painting "Oh Jerusalem." Brigitte had seen me admiring it in an Art shop and had surprised me with it on my birthday. It pictured Jesus, sitting on a mountainside, gazing down upon Jerusalem. I asked the five-year-old Kodi, "What do you think Jesus is thinking there."

His quick answer, "Why don't they listen to me?" The hair stood up on my forearms and the back of my neck.

I gave my children and grandchildren the same basic piece of advice. I emphasized, "Always remember, it's far easier to stay out of trouble then it is to get out of trouble. Staying out may be as simple as saying no. Getting out may require lawyers, doctors and lots of dollars."

Haworth gave me an elaborate retirement sendoff party.

The owner/president thanked me for my contribution to the growth and success of the company.

When my turn to speak arrived, I couldn't resist my urge to some humor. I spoke of my appreciation for the opportunities the company had provided me over my nineteen years. Then, I turned to the owner/president and said, "I especially want to thank you, sir. Shortly after I began employment, you sent me to a seminar on 'How to delegate work to others.' I learned well and I haven't, myself, done a day's work since."

The attendees burst into loud laughter. The aging president looked a bit taken aback but then managed an uncertain smile. He was a truly dignified gentleman who, although friendly and approachable, always looked serious.

I could never imagine him telling a joke. After all, he was an entrepreneur who built a billion-dollar business from a shop in his garage.

Because I retired the end of December, we soon left for our first retired winter in Arizona.

I had always given the maximum allowed amount to my company 401K plan and, with company contributions it had grown to a respectable sum.

I wasn't interested in the stock market, so I turned my and Brigitte's accounts over to a financial adviser to manage as individual IRAs.

I had always been blessed with enough money, so I wasn't interested in building wealth. I preferred living.

Brigitte and I began taking our early social security.

Brigitte also applied for and received a small monthly pension from Germany.

The pension was unexpected and would have gone uncollected except for a chance advertisement I saw in a Toronto newspaper when we visited Herbert and Gertrud. The service, headquartered in Australia, offered to investigate pension eligibility for ex citizens of Germany and if feasible, initiate the application for benefits. There was no charge if the effort was unsuccessful. If a pension were in fact successfully obtained, it would typically have a lump sum of accumulated unpaid benefits payable to the retiree. The Service's charge was a one-time payment of one half of the accumulated cash benefit. There was nothing to lose. Brigitte said, "Don't bother, I only worked five years and I didn't earn much." Her Brother and sister-in-law were both receiving German pensions sent to them in Toronto. They had applied through the German consulate. Gertrud said "Brigitte, if it's only ten dollars a month, take it. It's money and it's free."

I did some background checking to confirm that they were legitimate and not a scam.

I wrote the service and received their questionnaire.

I asked Brigitte if she had any work records. She had thrown everything away when she left Germany for her new life in America. I wrote a letter to them telling of Brigitte's Berlin meat market job and Frau Barkow's seamstress employment. They apparently wanted success more than Brigitte. They had their resources in Germany investigate and they were able to submit acceptable work record data. I had to send copies of Brigitte's German passport and her U.S. citizen certificate. After about three months Brigitte received a check for about seven thousand dollars. The Service was licensed by Germany and received their half directly.

Brigitte began getting a monthly direct deposit of approximately one hundred forty dollars which over time, through cost-of-living raises, became about one hundred seventy dollars. She soon began calling it her, "Casino money."

I received two company pensions and I immediately began taking a monthly, taxable payout from my IRA as it rose and fell with the market. We didn't let fear, greed or stock market concerns interfere with our living a comfortable, non-extravagant, interesting and prudent, retirement lifestyle.

We traveled, mostly by auto, through the States, Canada and Mexico. We didn't have reservations except on the rare occasions that we went with an organized tour.

The most memorable of these trips was the Canadian Maritimes in 1999. We experienced one serendipity after another. Traveling along the St Lawrence side of Quebec's Gaspe Peninsula we found picturesque fishing villages and enjoyed lobster at outdoor picnic tables. At the tip of the Gaspe peninsula, we planned to stay in the village of Perce. We wanted to walk out to the Perce Rock formation in the Gulf of Saint Lawrence, at low tide, and see the window formation in it. The small hotel there had no vacancies, but the proprietor told us he could rent us a suite in an adjacent condominium.

The price was surprisingly reasonable. It was a deluxe suite with all the conveniences including a large gas fireplace.

One wall was top to bottom glass and overlooked the Gulf of Saint Lawrence.

The remnants of hurricane Floyd had reached the Gaspe. Brigitte and I turned up the heat, turned on the big fireplace, snuggled together on a luxurious sofa, and watched a storm beat against the wall of windows. Yes, we had a bottle of Beaujolais wine which was popular in the Maritimes.

As we later snuggled in our soft and warm bed we agreed, we could never have planned all this.

The next morning, we learned that no one could walk to the Perce Rock. Floyd was blowing so hard that the morning tide didn't go out.

Prince Edward Island, New Brunswick, Cabot Island, and Nova Scotia were all wonderful experiences. We lived on seafood chowder, Mussels and of course Lobster.

We had many unplanned adventures and always felt secure in each other's company.

We complemented and enhanced each other's thinking and often came up with the same ideas.

Brigitte was the cooler one between us in an emergency, maybe from experiencing the war.

Once, when visiting the Mexican border, I mistakenly got into a traffic flow heading across the border and into Nogales, Mexico. It was four lanes, going one way.

Brigitte immediately said, "Don't cross the border, get over to the right, turn on your flashers, slow to a stop and then back up until you reach the intersection."

"I can't," I said. "It's all one way."

"Then let me drive," she said, "I'll do it."

I stopped and had my flashers on. Cars were swirling around me on my left and honking their horns.

I don't know how I managed. Oncoming traffic must have seen and took pity. Somehow, I backed far enough into an intersection to make a right-hand turn and escape the area.

Brigitte's border crossing concern was due to the bad experience her brother Herbert had several years earlier. He accidentally drove across the border from California into Tijuana, Mexico.

Herbert and Gertrud were detained several hours before finally being directed on how to return to California.

Herbert was too naive to offer to pay a "fine" to expedite his release.

In Arizona, family members, including Herb and Gertrud, frequently visited with us. Together we would often explore Arizona and the nearby states of California, New Mexico, Utah, and Nevada. Every state had its unique scenic beauty and attractions.

In Arizona, Brigitte and I, armed with county road maps, drove the back roads. We frequently came across signs, on the side of the road, warning of possibly encountering smuggling and other illegal activities in these remote areas, especially near the southern border.

Brigitte was fascinated with the historic legends of the American West and seemed fearless in exploring ghost towns, back roads, and remote, former mining areas.

When we were going to be out and about for the day, we usually took along a cooler with sandwiches, water, and a few beers.

On one such outing, we came upon an old graveyard.

It was obviously untended and was situated on the side of a gently rising hill. Old tombstones and stone borders marked the various graves. There were approximately a dozen vehicles, mostly pickup trucks, parked in an area near the beginning of the graves and along the dirt road.

A group of men, women, and children was gathered around a mound of fresh earth at an open new grave. Several were playing softly on guitars and singing in what I guessed was Spanish. Some younger men were resting their elbows on the back of a pickup and sipping bottles of beer.

Several were shoveling and obviously closing the grave.

We had parked a respectful distance away and, after watching for a while, Brigitte said, "Why don't you go talk to them and see what's going on."

Several of them had glanced at us several times, then, seemingly ignored us.

As I approached the group, one of them came toward me with a welcoming, friendly smile and greeted me.

I commented on what an unusual scene it was.

He nodded yes, then explained that this was, in former times, an active graveyard for several local families. He said most had left the area and it is now under the control of the Arizona Bureau of Land Management.

He told me an elderly patriarch of one of the families had recently died and had previously stated his wish to be buried in the old family cemetery. The family requested and received permission to conduct the burial.

He told me the Funeral Service delivered the casket to the site the family had selected, unloaded it, turned it over to the family and then left the scene.

The family and friends had dug the grave, conducted their ceremony, lowered the casket and were in the process of closing the grave as we came upon the scene.

The gentleman then said, "Come and walk with me."

He led me up the hill and amongst the graves. He told me the family surname and began pointing out the various old family graves of those who had preceded today's family patriarch.

Most of the graves had inscriptions with pertinent details of the life of the person including, in some cases, the type of death, some peaceful, some accidental and some violent.

The graves, all artistically enhanced, were suffering the ravages of time. Inscriptions and messages left by various means were becoming difficult to read.

I thanked the man for his kind attention and asked him to please extend my condolences to the family. As I walked quietly past the graveside gathering, I received numerous nods, mostly from the oldsters among them. We drove slowly away.

We were in the Springs for our second Winter when I met our neighbor Bob. He lived in the corner house across from ours. I was doing something in our yard when he rode up on his bicycle. He introduced himself. He was a retired Geologist. He and his wife, Sally, spent their summers at their home in Idaho.

He told me that he and another Springs neighbor, Jim, went out once a week, on Wednesdays, into the mountains and the desert prospecting for gold. He invited me to come along with them and give it a try. He said they used his four-wheel drive Jeep to manage the rugged terrain. I accepted his invitation.

I and Brigitte were invited to their next weekly Monday evening mining meeting. It would be on Bob and Sally's patio with the view of the Santa Rita mountains.

"Don't bring anything, just be there at 6:00 pm. Jim and his wife Jan will be there also."

When I told Brigitte, she was excited about getting to know some of our neighbors.

We went and met the two couples. Sally was an easy-going hostess and, had a snack prepared for us. Jim and Jan were an unpretentious couple from Ohio. Jan said she was originally from West Virginia and proud to be a hillbilly girl. We were all quickly at ease.

Bob asked what everyone wants for a drink. When we answered he said, "Good, we have it. Go in and help yourselves. There's a small bar in the kitchen with the fixings." Sally had a bucket of ice cubes set out for mixed drinks. A variety of liquors was there including a half gallon bottle of Vodka.

Jim and Bob spread out a Bureau of Land Management map which showed all the backroads and landmarks in the area where we would prospect. They selected an abandoned mine we would visit. They both had metal detectors that they explained they used to scan the pilings around the mine shafts.

They told me I would need to wear sturdy hiking boots, sturdy clothing and have a knapsack for a lunch and several quarts of water. They also said I should bring along my pistol. When I told them, I didn't own one they glanced at each other. Bob said, "If you decide you like it, and want to continue going, you should get a pistol and holster. There are mules out there carrying drugs from Sonora, Mexico and my Jeep might look tempting to them. Also, with the remote possibility of mountain lions, bears and occasional rattlesnakes a pistol is a comfort. There are also illegals, but they often are mostly women and children and they tend to try not to be seen. We do occasionally see border patrol vehicles and sometimes their helicopters drop down low to check us out. We wave at them and they usually quickly leave."

It all sounded interesting, so I bought the necessary boots, tough clothing and a knapsack.

The pistol would have to wait awhile. Bob and Jim could protect me from the perils of the Baboquivari mountains and the Sonoran Desert.

Brigitte and I began looking forward to the Monday evening mining meetings at Bob and Sally's patio.

They eventually turned into barbeques or informal, outdoor dinners with us taking turns buying the steaks or making the casseroles. The Vodka bottle got a lot of attention.

Bob and Sally were Idaho conservatives. This first came to light when Sally observed some Hispanics, possibly illegals, doing some work in our yard. Their boss, Jose, was a familiar sight in The Springs. He found work by word of mouth and by driving around in his old pickup truck looking for opportunities. I had flagged him down and asked him for an estimate to build us two small front and back entrance brick patios and to add some decorative gravel in our back yard. We signed a contract to be paid upon work completion. Jose had a reputation for good quality work and promptness. He acquired the materials and showed up with a crew of four Hispanics.

Brigitte saw them hard at work and quickly baked a three-layer chocolate Bundt cake.

Brigitte cooled it quickly in the refrigerator. She sliced it and set it out on our back patio table with a gallon of milk, forks, and paper cups and plates. She caught Jose's attention and indicated the cake was for them.

They soon took a break and were eating, drinking and enjoying the unexpected treat. As they were going back to work, one of the crew tapped on the patio door and said to Brigitte, "There is one slice of cake left. May I have it to take home to my Maria?"

Brigitte smiled, nodded yes, and got him a container.

Sally had witnessed all this from her kitchen window.

At our next get together she chastised Brigitte. "Why did you go through the trouble and give cake to those people? You know if you do things like that you spoil it for the rest of us who hire them. They will start to expect it."

Brigitte replied, "Sally, I feel sorry for them, I'm glad I done it. It made me happy seeing them enjoying themselves for a little while." Sally shook her head.

Brigitte and I both had sympathy for the Illegals who came up from the, mostly dry, Santa Cruz riverbed near our home. They followed the river from Sonora, Mexico to the Green Valley area where they typically exited. They then tried to make their way to Tucson and points North without being apprehended.

On several occasions, individuals had come to our home asking for food and water. Brigitte quickly made them a generous sandwich and after glasses of water, gave them a bottle of water to take with them.

One young man, in gratitude, pulled out a battered wallet, removed a picture card of "Our Lady of Guadalupe" and handed it to me. I've carried it in my wallet ever since.

Those fleeing from South of the border reminded us of the thousands of Eastern Europeans who we saw in camps around Berlin. They were hoping to get to West Germany and beyond, seeking a better and safer life.

Sally had chronic breathing problems and needed oxygen.

She had the face device and a long tube running to an oxygen tank. When she left the house, she carried a small tank with her.

Sally and I disagreed on various things and she complained to Brigitte that she had trouble knowing when I was serious. One day I found a chip of floor tile lying in the yard. It was a triangular piece only about an inch long, but it was colorful and caught my eye. I was doing some caulking when I spotted it, so I put a dab of caulk on it and stuck it on the tip of a large, pointed landscaping rock.

Sally stopped by to chat and spotted the tile sitting on the rock. "What's that," she asked pointing at it.

"I'm surprised you're asking," I said, "you must have not spotted the one in your yard. Every home here in Santa Rita Springs has one."

"What is it," she again demanded.

I said, "It's a compact high efficiency solar energy absorber. They radiate the electrical power that is used in all our homes."

"Then why the hell do I get an electrical bill every month," she said, and stormed off.

I think Sally tolerated me because at our weekly meetings she would ask me, not Bob, to go inside and refresh her drink. I would pour a generous amount of Vodka into her glass, with ice, and serve it undiluted. I liked Sally and I think she sensed it. Conservatives and Liberals can get along??

Our prospecting trips provided comradery. We would reach our destination on almost non-existent trails.

On occasion we had to gather rocks to fill in holes so the Jeep could continue. There were numerous abandoned mines. Typically, an opening surrounded by the excavated mounds of earth. Occasionally there would be the dilapidated remains of a miner's shack.

The BLM surrounded each mine shaft with a single strand of barbed wire. Each mine had a sign warning not to enter due to danger from poison gas, reptiles, and possible cave-ins.

Bob and Jim worked the pilings with their metal detectors. If they got a signal, they would dig a small pile from the spot and isolate it aside.

They would then reduce the small pile little by little until they found the cause of the signal.

It would typically be a rusty nail, a pop top, shoe eyelet, or some other artifact indicating the previous presence of humans.

The only gold we found was by panning in the occasional small trickling streams we found.

There, by patiently washing the small stones and dirt from our pans, we would reach the black, nitty gritty which contained the flour gold. You could best see it if it caught the sun and gleamed. We would take it to Jim who would verify its existence with his ten-power jeweler's loupe. He would then carefully suck it up with an eye dropper and place it in a test tube he carried for that purpose. My last look at the tube showed about two and a half inches of gold dust.

We didn't expect to get rich. It was the fresh air, exercise, and possible adventure that drew us.

After two or three hours we had enough. We'd meet back at the Jeep and have our lunch. Mine was usually already gone and Bob would give me one of his ever-present dill pickles.

In time we each had our nicknames. Jim had won a big jackpot at one of the Casinos along the Gulf Coast, so he was "Diamond Jim." Bob's prostate surgery had increased his urgency, so we occasionally had to stop to let him receive himself. Jim said Bob was like a coyote always marking his turf. Bob was, "Coyote Bob."

I didn't want to use a metal detector so, while they had their heads down detecting, I would be looking around spotting things and pointing them out. I became, "Eagle Eye Lou."

One summer, at home in Ohio, Jim had tee-shirts made for us. Emblazoned on the front was, *"The Fresh Air Mining Company."* There was a picture of a mine entrance and a glittering pile of gold ore. There were also three prospectors, each one had one of our new nicknames above him.

There was a small settlement, named Arivaca, along our normal route from Green Valley. We stopped in at the La Gitana bar which always had their colorful, local clientele. They got to know us and invited us into their conversations. We received a lot of advice on where the best *washes* were to detect for gold. Occasionally someone would run home and return with one or two small nuggets to show us.

Bob, our retired geologist, would look them over lovingly with his powerful jeweler's loupe and confirm,

"Yup, they're the real thing."

Our La Gitana acquaintances had pretty much dropped out of society. They were mostly bachelor retirees and Viet Nam veterans. They might pick up odd jobs but were mostly surviving on Social Security and Disability payments. They lived simply and basically.

Across the street was the Mercantile which did a steady business in sandwiches and microwaved entrees.

They accepted each other "as is" and were always quick to help each other. Whenever a benefit was scheduled to help someone in need, the La Gitana was packed with locals ready to help as best they could from their own meager resources.

Many people in Green Valley heard of Arivaca but were afraid to go there. It was in fact peaceful.

A lot of marijuana trafficked through that area but it when on quietly.

One evening I took Brigitte there for her first visit.

I ordered us each a draft beer and we sat at a table.

Brigitte looked around at the rustic and colorful.

surroundings and the various wall signs. The characters sitting around the bar would not inspire a feeling of safety with their long, unkempt hair and beards.

A grizzled older man must have thought Brigitte looked uneasy. He slid off his bar stool and walked over to Brigitte. He said, "Ma'am, you don't have to be afraid, you're in Arivaca, you're safe here." We enjoyed many visits there.

In the early to mid-2000's we often saw groups of illegals, mostly pitiful looking women and children, sitting in groups on the side of the road to Arivaca. Seeing them, I couldn't despise them. I couldn't help feeling affection and sympathy for them and, I admired their courage. After an exceedingly difficult and dangerous journey over mountains and desert they had been apprehended by the Border Patrol. They were waiting for the buses that would return them to Mexico through the Nogales port of entry. The buses were contracted by the U.S. and, at that time period, were a common sight traveling South on Interstate 19, loaded with illegals. Some entity had found favor and was awarded that lucrative busing contract.

Our Southern border is a challenge. How to deal with the unending stream of those seeking to find a better life in the U.S.A. is thus far an unsolved problem. Helping the countries to develop, which they are leaving, can be a step in curbing the desire to flee. I pray that God will lead us to an effective and humane solution.

It was in the year 2005 that my Brigitte told me something was wrong. She noticed a slight tremor had begun in her left hand. It didn't cause any problems and wasn't of concern.

Of greater concern was that she was beginning to have trouble initiating movement to simply walk.

Her personal physician referred her to a neurologist.

After several minutes of examination and observing her movements, he diagnosed Parkinson's disease.

He prescribed a low dose of Carbidopa/Levodopa (Sinemet) to attempt to ease the, so far, mild symptoms.

As we drove home, Brigitte said, "Well, my beloved, we know what's ahead for us, but we also know I still have some good years. Let's just keep on living and make the best of them." She continued, "With your help, I'll keep on going to the best of my ability and let's continue enjoying the same things as long as we can."

Then she said, "When the time comes, when we can no longer handle it, and we know that time will eventually come, just help me to go peacefully. Don't let them feed me through the stomach and make me "just exist" the way my brother Herbert did for his last two years."

Brigitte's older brother Herbert was diagnosed with Parkinson's at age forty-seven. He lived with it, with declining quality of life, for twenty-eight years.

We had always been closest with Herbert and Gertrud. Over the years, we visited back and forth between Michigan and Toronto. We vacationed together all over the US and Canada.

Herb convinced me that he and I should take up archery hunting. We each bought a Fred Bear re-curve bow.

Herb came to Michigan every year to spend a week with me, at the Buckhorn property, during the deer season.

Herb had to kind of drag his polio-affected leg along but, with his Germanic determination, he kept up and never asked for respite. We had occasional success which was anti-climactic to the joy of being in God's beautiful fall woods and occasionally sipping an Asbach Uralt German brandy which Herb brought along.

Buckhorn Lodge's property was seventy-nine acres because the previous owner held back the Northwest corner acre when he sold to the Lodge. He had planned to build a retirement home there. One Fall we spotted a For Sale sign on that corner. Herb said, "Let's buy it!" We did and Herb named it, "The Hawk's Nest."

On a family vacation in Rheinlander, Wisconsin, Herbert confided in me that he had been diagnosed with Parkinson's disease. We were sitting together in a small rowboat, fishing. I hadn't heard much about the disease at the time, but it sounded ominous. The beautiful lake we were boating on suddenly lost its charm. Herb was forty-nine at the time. Herb bravely challenged the disease for every bit of the life that it slowly took from him.

He would get frustrated when he would drop something or would freeze up and couldn't initiate movement, but he never quit trying to his dying day.

Herb lived with the slowly worsening effects for twenty-eight years. His last two years, he was fully immobile and nourished and hydrated artificially. Herbert could no longer speak or write but he was aware, recognized us, and could respond to questions by nodding his head slightly.

We drove to Toronto and visited Herb quite regularly. In good weather, the staff would place Herb in a wheelchair, and I would wheel him outside and around the grounds.

I would talk about our family and he would listen and nod. He liked a good joke, and his shoulders would shake with his silent laughter.

The Canadian health care system served Herbert admirably.

He was well cared for, first in hospitals for falls and fractures, then, eventually, in an assisted living facility. He and Gertrud were never concerned about health insurance or health care costs. Herbert was offered and accepted the, then state of the art, deep brain stimulation operation to alleviate Parkinson's symptoms. It was marginally effective.

For several more years, Herbert and Gertrud were able to travel with us. We would rent a large four door sedan with a big trunk for Herb's wheelchair, and all our luggage.

Herbert died peacefully in 2010 at age seventy-seven. Herbert's wife Gertrud had faithfully taken a cab every day to visit Herbert wherever he was being cared for and was with him when he died.

Gertrud was a simple woman and turned to us for help.

We visited regularly to Toronto during Herbert's last two years and after, until Gertrud's death.

We took Gertrud on mini trips around the Toronto area and tried to cheer her but she kept asking, "Why didn't he take me with him?"

Gertrud now lived alone in their Toronto home. Their son Reinhard had died at age forty-one of throat cancer which was attributed to his heavy smoking.

Gertrud had lived a hard early life. She was raised on her family's farm in German occupied Poland. At age fourteen, Gertrud was going down a lane to the neighboring farm to barter some produce. A vehicle of advancing Russians captured her and sent her, along with others they had captured, to Siberia to work harvesting Peat moss, which the Russians used for fuel.

There, Gertrud slept on straw in crude barracks with long wooden racks for sleeping. The prisoners ate meager meals mostly of soup made from root crops.

She woke one morning to find a young lady she had befriended, lying dead next to her. The friend was fragile and had succumbed to exposure and malnutrition.

Gertrud was sturdy enough to survive several years until the war's end. She was released and found her way eventually to Berlin where she found work as a housemaid. There she met and married Brigitte's brother Herbert.

With Herbert gone, Gertrud was alone in Toronto. She was financially secure in their paid for home and with her company pension and Canadian Social Security, so she refused to move into assisted living.

One night as she sat alone watching television, a heavy thunderstorm hit Toronto and the power went out.

Having lived through the noise of war, Gertrud was always very afraid of thunder. Frightened, Gertrud decided to go down to the basement and sleep where the thunder was less noticeable. In the dark, she missed a step and fell to the basement floor. She crawled to the bed, which had been used by Herbert, but was unable to raise herself into it. She pulled off the covers from the bed and used them and the pillow as she lay on the floor.

Gertrud remained on the cold basement floor for a day and a half until a concerned neighborhood friend, who Gertrud had entrusted with a key, entered the house and found her.

The neighbor called emergency and then notified us in Michigan. She had our address and phone number in case of such emergency. We had gone out to dinner several times with her in Toronto, so she was comfortable calling us.

We immediately drove to Toronto. We found Gertrud in Intensive Care at North York General Hospital. She had contracted double pneumonia and was on a ventilator.

At eighty-four years of age, her vital signs indicated the end was near. Gertrud recognized us and was able to nod her head *yes* or *no* to our questions.

The attending staff asked us to ask Gertrud if she would agree to removing the ventilator and try breathing on her own. They clarified that she may recover and breath on her own or, she may die of pneumonia.

Now that we were there and she no longer felt alone, Gertrud wanted the ventilator removed. She was ready to go to be with Herbert and her son Reinhard.

Gertrud was kept comfortable and peaceful under what the Canadians called *palliative care.*

We stayed with her most of the next couple of days and were with her when she peacefully stopped breathing. While we were with Gertrud in Toronto, Brigitte and I quietly celebrated our fifty-fifth anniversary.

We stayed in Gertrud's home as we made the necessary arrangements. I soon would have to begin the long and complicated process of settling Gertrud's will and estate. I would be working from the United States but under Canadian law and using a Canadian lawyer. It was a long period of phone and Email communications.

I learned a lot about Canadian estate law. By doggedly personally petitioning the court I was able to avoid paying a large fee for an estate bondsman despite my being a non-resident Executor. I had to work around the advice of my Canadian lawyer. The estate is settled. My three terms of Business Law under the GI Bill gave me the confidence to doggedly see it through. After all expenses were paid, the balance of the estate was divided evenly between Brigitte, and her brother Gunther who resided in Berlin. All was done according to Herb and Gertrud's legal will on file in Toronto.

We brought Gertrud's cremains back to Michigan and buried them with Herbert's near his beloved Buckhorn Lodge.

There is a large boulder in the corner of the woods and on it are memorial plaques for both Herbert and Gertrud.

Their son Reinhard's ashes are with his wife in Toronto.

Herbert had said that he wanted his ashes spread on the Northwest corner acre, adjacent to the Buckhorn Lodge property. I was going to do it but my son Michael, now grown and with a son of his own, said, "No way, Dad. I'm going to get a large boulder and you're going to get an appropriate memorial plaque to put on it. Uncle Herb loved trains and deer hunting so make sure the plaque has a deer on one end and a train on the other."

My son Michael spent several weeks with Gertrud and Herbert one summer in Toronto. Herbert wanted Mike's help with some maintenance projects on their home.

They argued about German craftsmanship versus Yankee ingenuity. Herbert liked Michael's entrepreneurial spirit and they bonded.

Getting and placing the boulder was quite a project but with Mike as "ramrod" we got it done. When Gertrud died, we added her "Faithful Wife" plaque below Herb's plaque.

Brigitte and I continued to divide our time between Michigan and Arizona.

In the Green Valley and Tucson area, there were several large, modern casinos with excellent restaurants. We went to them for dinners and occasional Sunday Champagne breakfasts. Once, as we were waiting for a table, Brigitte put twenty dollars into a hallway slot machine.

She was betting two dollars at a time in the dollar machine. On about the fourth pull, she won eighty dollars.

Our table was now ready, so she cashed out and had ninety-two dollars. "That was fun," she said.

I didn't think much of it at the time. Brigitte had always insisted on waiting in the car if I ran into a casino for a half hour. She didn't like the smoke, so she would take up her knitting while she waited.

We usually had plenty of social gatherings and activities to keep us interested and entertained. But, on the occasions when nothing was planned, Brigitte began to say, "Let's go to the casino."

The Parkinson's was slowing her down and she had recently been diagnosed with Chronic Lymphocytic Leukemia (CLL).

The casino was easy, effortless entertainment.

Brigitte reasoned she really had nothing else to spend "her money" on. She wasn't gambling away needed funds. When I mildly objected to the twenty-dollar bills disappearing into the slot machines, Brigitte invited me to go get myself a beer and mind my own business.

Brigitte, of course, enjoyed winning but it was not as important as the play itself.

She said, "Lou, when I'm sitting at a slot machine all my physical concerns and discomforts are forgotten. And, I often have friendly talk with someone on an adjacent machine." The casino became one of our things to do.

In 2010, Brigitte had Orthopedic reconstructive surgery to alleviate severe pain in her left foot. Our retired M.D. brother-in-law had advised strongly against it. "Do your best with orthopedic footwear," he advised. He cautioned that recovery would be difficult due to Parkinson's complications.

He also warned of the real dangers of infection and possible blood clots. And, he added that the operations frequently fail to correct the problem.

We met with the surgeon and discussed these concerns.

He told us Parkinson's disease was no reason to suffer with foot pain and reduced mobility. He said, "We will take good care of you." We proceeded with the surgery.

All the bad things our brother-in-law cautioned us about happened, including the blood clot in her left calf. I had the unpleasant task of giving her anti-coagulant injections in her stomach, subcutaneously, for several days. Then for several months, we had to deal with the warfarin regimen.

Ultimately, another surgeon had to do left foot surgery to remove two screws from the heel which were installed as part of the reconstruction surgery and were causing irritation and pain. She also required further surgery to straighten out her left big toe.

Brigitte never recovered her previous mobility and balance and found it necessary to use a walker.

In September 2014, Brigitte was using her walker in our bedroom when it scooted away from her before she could set the wheel brakes. She crashed to the floor. I came running just as she grabbed her right foot, which was at a ninety-degree angle, and twisted it back in place.

She said, "Help me up onto the seat of the walker and call 911." She was sure the ankle was broken.

At the hospital, she had emergency surgery to repair her right ankle which was fractured in three places.

Between the bad left foot, the broken ankle, and the effects of Parkinson's, extensive physical therapy treatment was unable to get Brigitte back on her feet again.

We now entered the stage of needing the wheelchair for all transfers from bed to bath, to chair, to auto, etc.

Through it all, Brigitte was upbeat, and we still looked forward to every day even though they were becoming more demanding as the Parkinson's decline accelerated.

2015 was our last year to travel to Arizona and spend a winter with our friends there. Travel difficulties became prohibitive when Brigitte could no longer manage a handicap bathroom stall on her own with a walker.

I had to now wheel her into a stall and help her. I'd ask some woman to stand at the door and explain our need to anyone seeking to enter. As we exited, there was usually a short line of waiting women, mostly smiling understandingly.

On one occasion, I heard a woman proclaim loudly, "I don't care who is in there, I got to go!"

Through the open stall door, I saw a young woman run into the adjoining stall and slam down the seat. Almost immediately, I could hear that she really had to pee desperately.

The American Disability Act was a godsend in many ways but there were still too few of the family bathrooms.

These conveniences allowed a caregiver to wheel their charge in, lock the door, and help them with their needs in complete privacy.

Hotels had handicap rooms which were obviously not designed by a knowledgeable caregiver. Beds were too high, toilet seats too low, doors opened in the way of a wheelchair, showers had tubs, basins had no knee space, and grab bars weren't well planned or located.

With little or no added cost, standard hotel rooms could all be designed to accommodate most stages of disabilities in the elderly who prefer convenience and safety to "fancy." I'm confident they would soon become attractive rooms of choice for elderly travelers and a boon to the chain wise enough to implement them.

Our annual trip, to Arizona and back, had become too difficult so we had to stop.

In 2016, our Arizona home stood empty for the first time. Movement in general was becoming more difficult. Brigitte could no longer practice her pastime of knitting and crocheting. She would try but soon give up in frustration. At one time, she could do them without looking. Transferring food from her plate was slow and swallowing became difficult.

The neurologist prescribed from his arsenal of Parkinson's medicines that had evolved over the years.

Brigitte was prescribed a combination of Sinemet, Artane and Mirapex.

The neurologist saw Brigitte briefly once a month. I saw her continuously every day. I observed which medicines did what. I quickly learned which one(s) helped improve movement, and which one(s) helped control tremor. I also learned that accumulative buildup could occur causing heightened negative side effects such as confusion and illusions and uncontrollable upper body and head movements. By continually closely observing cause and effect, I became adept at adjusting doses by splitting tablets or skipping doses. It was effective and Brigitte was kept functional, lucid and reasonably comfortable.

Despite our challenging caregiver and patient roles, we kept our humor and still looked forward to every day together. We even managed occasional trips to our several Michigan Indian casinos. I'd wheel Brigitte to a favorite machine then stroll around while keeping an eye on her.

A nice thing about the casinos was that they all had nice clean, well kept, family restrooms.

The physical trauma of the broken ankle and the foot surgery resulted in Brigitte developing lymphedema in both lower legs.

I was taught how to do massage therapy and compression wrapping to treat and control the swelling.

We had our daily routine well established. In the morning, I'd help Brigitte out of bed and into her bathroom where I'd give her whatever assistance she required. I would then wheel her into the living room and transfer her to her easy chair. She'd watch and I'd listen to the morning news on TV while I made a simple breakfast.

I had installed ramps so I could wheel her outside on our deck or into the van for a ride. Evenings, after we had supper, I'd put her in her chair for our evening TV news and shows. She enjoyed *Jeopardy* and *Wheel of Fortune.*

Often, when I'd be in the kitchen doing supper dishes, she'd call to me, "Hon, let those dishes be and come and watch with me."

I'd answer, "Remember all those years when I would call to you, Hon, leave those dishes and come watch with me?"

She would usually answer, "If I sit now, I'll just have to do them later, just wait, I'll be there soon."

I'd then say, "Now it's the same for me."

Now I realize with regret, I should have left the dishes and joined her. I could have done dishes after she was in bed for the night.

The night of April 19, 2017, Brigitte woke me saying, "Something is wrong, I can't move my legs."

"Don't worry," I said. "It's probably just a medication problem. We'll up your dose in the morning."

The next morning as I sat her up and swung her legs out of the bed to help her into the wheelchair, she immediately fell backward. I said, "You have to help me, Hon. Sit until I can get the gait belt around you and help stand you up."

She tried and collapsed back again.

"I'm sorry," she said. "I can't, something has happened, something is wrong. We need to call 911."

For the last several weeks, our ability to cope had declined noticeably. It was getting physically strenuous. I prayed for guidance on how we are to proceed.

First on the scene after the 911 call was a tall, robust sheriff's deputy followed quickly by the ambulance crew.

I explained to them that Brigitte had lost her upper body strength. The deputy exclaimed, "Oh, it's a urinary tract infection."

"We're familiar with UTIs," I said. "Our concern is her sudden loss of strength."

The deputy replied, "Oh, a UTI can cause a loss of strength in an elderly woman."

I wanted to ask him if he was qualified to make a medical diagnosis, but I learned long ago to keep my eyes on the goal, so I didn't. I wanted friendly cooperation to get her safely to Emergency. They lifted Brigitte from the bed and took her in the ambulance.

I quickly put together a few things and followed.

It took me a few minutes to check Brigitte in at Admitting. It was the twentieth day of April 2017.

When they took me to her room, the deputy had apparently rendered his diagnosis. A nattily dressed doctor, sitting on the foot of her bed, told me they were treating her, with an IV, for a UTI. I told him that was not our concern. We called 911 because of her sudden loss of upper body strength. He smiled amiably and said, "I'm a hospital doctor. We know a bit more than the ordinary doctors. We'll take proper care of your wife."

The weekend began and I never saw that doctor again. I stayed at Brigitte's bedside.

On Sunday, April 23rd, a female doctor, doing weekend rounds, entered Brigitte's room and chatted with my son and me. I briefly described the recent events that led us to Emergency.

The doctor looked closely at Brigitte and said, "I believe she has had a stroke; the corner of her mouth has a very slight droop, and she is drooling slightly there."

She raised Brigitte's left arm and asked her to hold it up. It fell immediately. The left leg reacted the same. Brigitte was sent immediately for a brain scan which confirmed she had suffered a mild stroke. Happily, she could still talk. As I held her hand, she looked at me and said, "Please stay by me." I stayed by her day and night.

In America, physical therapists, working in concert with health insurance companies, not doctors, determine the length of treatment and care for ordinary insured individuals. On April 25th, at the urging of the hospital physical therapist and the insurance company, Brigitte was discharged from the hospital and sent on to recover in a skilled nursing facility. As I was sitting in the hospital room waiting for the ambulance to come and move Brigitte, a nurse came and knelt by me, put her hand on my knee, and said, "Lou, I'm sorry but I must tell you, Brigitte will never come home again."

My youngest son, Michael, asked me if I had arranged for a priest to administer the sacrament of the anointing of the sick. I was so involved with Brigitte's physical care I didn't think of it.

Michael drove Father Peter Omogo, of Nigerian descent, from his home parish in Montague to Holland. Brigitte received reconciliation, communion and anointing from Father Peter. She was visibly now at peace.

I am forever thankful to Michael and Father Peter.

Brigitte now could no longer swallow food nor drink. Because the skilled nursing facility was not authorized to use IVs, they attempted to hydrate Brigitte through drip needles inserted in her lower belly fat. Brigitte said the scruffy male nurse who inserted them was a "leering creep" who took unnecessarily long at the task. She refused further use of that treatment.

It would be nice if male nurses took care of males and female nurses took care of females, especially for intimate care.

I continued to stay by Brigitte sleeping on a pile of blankets the attending staff kindly provided. My two children who lived in Holland also stayed by her many hours.

My daughter often urged me to go home and jump in bed at home for at least a couple of hours. She would stay with Mom until I returned. I tried to shower and shave at least every other day.

After approximately fourteen days, the physical therapist at the skilled nursing facility regretfully reported that Brigitte was not responding to therapy therefore our health insurance would no longer cover her stay.

We were now on our own for care and lodging. We were advised to involve hospice in Brigitte's care.

Our children found a nice elder care home with a small, private suite that had a large bedroom and sitting room with kitchenette. There was also a private bathroom and, although Brigitte could no longer manage the use of it, I could.

We moved in together on May 11th.

I had a bed right next to Brigitte's hospice bed. It was a welcome change. In the hospital and skilled nursing facility, I slept on the floor or in a chair next to her bed. The nurses and attendants had given me blankets and pillows and stepped carefully past me as they checked on Brigitte throughout the night. Occasionally I was awakened by the thump of a pillow hitting me. It was Brigitte checking to assure herself that I was there. I'd give her a hug and say, "I'm here, please let me sleep."

Here, we could fall asleep holding hands and I could quickly react and get help if needed. I also was a knowledgeable patient advocate which made a significant difference in Brigitte's care.

On Mother's Day 2017, we had a party in our little suite. Our children, their spouses and our grandchildren were there. We sipped some wine, joked, and each of them had a chance to hold Brigitte's hand and visit with her. One of the grandchildren brought along a small, well behaved dog. Brigitte enjoyed holding it and petting it. She always liked and was at ease with animals of all sorts.

It was a long but happy day for Brigitte.

In the evening, after they had left and we were alone, Brigitte took my hand and said, "Isn't it nice that they all had a chance to say goodbye." Tears welled up in my eyes, as they are now as I write this. It was the first time that she openly acknowledged that she knew the end was near.

She wasn't afraid but she was worried about me. I had heard my oldest son Jack say to her, "Don't worry, Mom, we'll all take good care of Dad." She had nodded, obviously relieved.

Monday was a pleasant sunny day. I asked the staff to use the patient hoist to take Brigitte from her bed and place her in the special semi-reclining wheelchair that Hospice had provided. Brigitte had said it would be nice to go outside. The facility was away from town and nicely located in what looked like a large grassy meadow.

I took her outside in the wheelchair and slowly pushed her along the paved walkways. As I was heading back toward the entrance, Brigitte motioned me to her with her hand. I stopped pushing, went to her, and leaned over to her.

She looked at me at me with those lovely brown eyes and said, "Hon, can we please get us a nice little doggie?"

A lump came in my throat. "Yes, I said, that's a good idea, we'll get us one." She looked pleased. In retrospect, I believe Brigitte wanted the "doggie" actually for companionship for me after she was gone.

I took her back to the room and the staff soon had her comfortably back in her bed.

During the week, the hospice nurse told me the end was near. Brigitte had ceased any attempt to eat or drink and her medications were halted. Her body was slowly shutting down. She stopped talking and slept peacefully and quietly.

I knelt next to her bed, rested my head on her bosom and held her and hugged her as often and as long as I could.

My son Martin and daughter Dierdre who lived in Holland, spent their spare hours supporting me and watching Mom while I occasionally ran home to check on the house and change clothes. My daughter laundered all her mom's nightgowns and kept a ready supply in her bedside closet.

Dierdre spent all her available time at her mom's bedside moistening her mouth and removing and wiping away the mucus which would accumulate in the lower corner of Brigitte's mouth.

During the night, I would reach across and hold Brigitte's hand until my arm grew tired or I fell asleep.

Occasionally, I would be treated by a soft hand squeeze.

She no longer spoke but I was told she could hear.

Saturday evening, May 20th, I sat on my bed and looked at Brigitte sleeping peacefully. I knew there could no longer be a recovery, so I prayed that God bless my Brigitte with a peaceful death.

An attendant entered the room and saw me sitting there. She asked me if I would like my bed pushed tight against Brigitte's. I decided no, because I needed the little space in between to get in and out of my bed which was against the wall on the other side. I kissed Brigitte goodnight and got into my bed.

I fell asleep Saturday night praying my rosary and asking that Brigitte suffer no discomfort or fear.

I woke suddenly and sat up. I glanced at my watch. It was 2:30 am Sunday morning.

I got out of bed, leaned over Brigitte and spoke her name. Brigitte pursed up her lips ever so slightly.

I put my arms around her, raised her head slightly, and kissed her. Her lips were so soft, and she was so warm.

I laid her back on her pillow and waited and listened for her to take a breath. As I looked at her, I was struck by how beautiful she looked. She just seemed to glow with what could only be peace and joy.

I thought, *Jesus is taking her soul to eternity.*

I held Brigitte in my arms again for the last time, kissed her once more, and said, "Goodbye my darling, I love you, I will miss you, and I will find you again in heaven." I laid her carefully back down. I saw her big comb on the windowsill. I took it, combed her hair back for the last time and went to find an attendant. The attendant immediately notified Hospice.

I called Dierdre and Martin. Despite the early morning hour, they were both there quickly. They each gave their mom a goodbye hug and kiss.

The Hospice nurse was also quickly there. She examined Brigitte thoroughly and pronounced her deceased at 3:29a.m.

Later in the morning, as I, my son Martin, and my daughter Dierdre left the facility to go home, we walked past a row of shrubbery. The bushes were alive with a flock of chickadees chirping and dancing around in the branches. That was the kind of scene Brigitte loved.

It was a beautiful Spring morning, May 21st, 2017.

What Now?

Now, three years later, at age eighty-four, I'm alone with wonderful memories of my life with my German Fraulein, turned American, Brigitte. But also, with occasional pangs of guilt.

I was so busy caring for her the last several years, did I tell her often enough how much I loved her?

Even now I look around our large yard and see the results of her work. Long heavy-duty rubber lawn edgings separating the lawn from her flower beds. How did she do it? A yard full of shrubs, planted by her over the years.

A floor of patio stones leveled and placed beneath our large rear patio. Circular curbing placed around our ornamental tree trunks. Brigitte had done the same sorts of things in our previous home in Whitehall. All done while I sat in an air-conditioned office.

And, she would still have the pickup packed and ready so we could head north for a weekend at the Buckhorn cabin where we would often sit around bonfires with our, mostly farmers, local friends. We'd drink beer and talk and joke while soft music, mostly slow country, would play on someone's portable in the background. The skies would be loaded with stars in the surrounding darkness. Those are blessed who have experienced those kinds of times and those kinds of friends.

Now, I wondered, *did I really let her know how much I appreciated her wisdom and skill in raising our family and caring for our home. Did I tell her what a great partner she was?*

Does any man ever do these things right or do we all learn and appreciate the value of a good woman and partner too late, and just go through life taking them for granted?

I don't ask for signs but since I lost my Brigitte, I've been blessed with several.

I had been praying God to tell her I loved her and missed her, because I felt I hadn't said "I love you" enough to her in her last months. After she had been gone about five months, I had a vivid dream. We were in my parent's home at the top of the stairs where they had the room for us when we arrived from Germany, she was suddenly standing there and I thought, *Now I can tell her!* I wrapped my arms around her in a tight embrace and said, "I love you; I love you so much." She was then out of my arms and standing to the side.

She said clearly, "I know you loved me, you always did your best for me." Those were her only words, and she was gone.

I woke in the morning and, remembering, immediately said, "Thank you for this gift of reassurance." I saw this dream as a comforting answer to my prayers.

Then, a short while back, I had a spiritual experience so vivid and real that, as it ended, I thought, *No one but me can believe this. So, I won't bother to mention it.*

But now I will share it.

The spiritual experience I had was not a dream. Another concern I had was a feeling that during our sixty years together I had not done as good a job as I should have in helping my Brigitte to grow in faith, hope and love. I asked God to blame me if she was not strong enough in those beliefs and to forgive her. Although I was blessed to see her beautifully at peace as she took her last breath I often wondered, *Is she okay? Is she safely with Jesus?*

This particular morning, I awoke and started to turn to get out of bed. As I looked toward the window, I was startled to see my Brigitte there and smiling a most beautiful smile. I blurted out, "My gosh, it's you, you're not dead; but I know you are dead." She was not solid, human flesh but still, beautifully and happily there before me. I noticed her hair, which was shoulder length and permed as from earlier days. Then, she was gone.

It was real, Brigitte was there. It was not a dream.

She never spoke a word but had warmly smiled at me and radiated peace and joy. I thought, *Again, God has favored me with His answer to my concern.*

I've thought about this experience. I went online to question the various Christian religions' thoughts on spiritual visions and ghosts.

All Christian sects seem to agree that actively seeking to conjure up, converse with, or contact spirits through fortune tellers, spiritualists, or any means is immoral. However, if God chooses, as He has in the Bible, to use spirits and angels, to His purpose, to visit humans, it is within His power to do so.

It seems my experience is not unusual, and God can send us spirits to reassure us that our departed loved ones are safe and happy if He so chooses. I had this happy spiritual experience and I know I was awake and of clear mind.

My last special dream experience with Brigitte is what I genuinely believe was a foretaste of Heaven. In this short but very intense dream, Brigitte and I were standing close together and "shining like the sun." We were sharing an indescribable state of absolute joy and unbounded contentment. No earthly experience or state of being can begin to compare to that momentary, heavenly ecstasy I experienced. I must strive to get there!

My life, which happened by God's providence, more than it was planned by me, has been very blessed.

I can't help but think about those, especially the unbelievably resilient little ones, who suffer hunger and homelessness. The beautiful faces of the suffering children still seem to hold out hope that something better lies ahead. Can we just ignore them all, and write them off?

I pray that someday we will learn to overcome our insatiable greed, find ways to better share life's blessings, and thus, improve the lives of those now being left behind.

My closing "Old Guy's" advice; If you want to be happy, find your life partner. Love and respect him or her more than you do yourself. Commit your life to making your partner feel loved, safe, and secure. Forsake greed and treasure contentment. Confide and trust in your God, and you will live the 23rd Psalm all your lives.

Now, I continue to run the race, an imperfect man, relying on faith, hope and, love. I thank God that I can still go up north with my sons and, prowl the cold, clear streams of Michigan, in quest of my limit of five brook trout.

My four adult children trust me, thus far, with my independence. They do, however, linger nearby, especially my dear daughter Dierdre, keeping a watchful eye on Dad.

Brigitte, be patient, pray for me and the kids, and I'll see you soon.

All my love, your, *"Louiechen."*

CPSIA information can be obtained
at www.ICGtesting.com
Printed in the USA
FSHW022207050721
82941FS

9 781649 793157